How to Build & Use Greenhouses

Created and designed by the editorial staff of ORTHO Books

Written by T. Jeff Williams

Art Direction by James Stockton

Illustrations by Ron Hildebrand

Photography by Michael Landis

Front and back cover photographs by John Blaustein

Additional photography by
William Apton
Tony Howarth
Fred Kaplan

W0007865

Introduction

The world of greenhouses is a world of magic. Harvest garden fresh tomatoes in March, grow poinsettias for December.

Stepping into a greenhouse for the first time is like stepping into another world—and a magical one at that. There's a feeling of following Alice down the rabbit hole and suddenly appearing in the Queen of Hearts' exotic garden. It may be freezing and snowing outside but once inside the greenhouse you are transported to the steamy, languid tropics. Around you may be clusters of orchids, those delicate natives of the Amazon jungle that have no right to be blooming in the depths of winter. But there they are, thanks to the greenhouse.

Orchids amidst snow flurries is just one thing a greenhouse can do for you. It creates a special atmosphere where all kinds of plants and flowers can flourish year-round, and so can your peace of mind.

There is also considerable satisfaction in harvesting a basket laden with lettuce, radishes and snow peas for a garden-fresh salad in February while your neighbors are bemoaning the high cost of such produce —*if* it's even available. Extra satisfaction comes if you've built the greenhouse yourself. Many plans for construction, plus details on how to make a greenhouse operate at peak efficiency, are in this book.

But this is much more than a book about greenhouses. It's a detailed look at controlling the environment to make your plants grow where nature wouldn't let them without your help. If you live in the windswept Great Plains, for instance, Mother Nature didn't intend to have her tomato plants or zinnias sprouting in March. But there are ways to fool Mother Nature, like starting those tomatoes and zinnias early—and snugly protected—inside cold frames or hot beds.

And in the summer, when the sun makes it too uncomfortable for you to enjoy your patio at midday, you can change the environment by building a shade porch or lath house out there. It can be attached to the wall of your house to expand your living area. A myriad of flowering plants will thrive in the cool, indirect light under this structure.

Your own house or apartment is a controlled environment by itself. But in many cases, it is too dry and there is not enough light for plants. These problems can be overcome, however, and you'll find many tips on how to do so in this book. You can even redesign whole rooms with the needs of plants in mind. Even if you live in a crowded place, don't despair. There is more space around you than you think: look up, look down, look in closets and along narrow windowsills, almost anywhere that can be widened to hold plants.

Opposite, from outside a greenhouse, silhouettes of winter-protected sago palms are visible. Other winter-time possibilities inside a greenhouse include: above, geraniums trained into standards; left, warm colors of chrysanthemums.

At this point, you might be thinking you really don't want to be bothered with the care and feeding of a jungle, still you want something green and growing around you. The terrarium might be just the answer. Small and delicate plants will thrive in this miniature greenhouse. Once it's planted, with the rain cycle established, you mostly sit back and enjoy.

For the more adventurous growers, there is a whole section devoted to setting up and operating a hydroponic garden. Those converted to soilless growing—and they number in the thousands—claim their vegetables grow faster than in regular gardens, and even taste better. A hydroponic system is ideally run in a greenhouse but it can be made to work in an apartment under fluorescent lights.

Light is critical for making plants grow, outdoors or indoors. The indoor light garden is a rapidly expanding phenomenon in this country where

Built in 1851, London's famous Crystal Palace was one of the world's most elaborate greenhouses. It housed numerous tropical and exotic plants collected by plant explorers. Its construction exemplified significant improvements in the manufacture of glass and steel.

whole banks of plants and flowers, particularly the African violet, are being grown under lights. The wonderful thing about a light garden is that it can be put in the darkest of places.

If you're aiming at the big satisfaction of building your own greenhouse, there are many styles to choose from in this book and one of them should fit your needs, whether you live in Minnesota or Alabama. Whatever style you choose, give careful consideration to the section on solar greenhouses. There you'll find suggestions that can help you sharply reduce heating costs. This applies even if you already have a greenhouse, because there are several ways to improve its performance.

The greenhouse that you build will link you to centuries of tradition in man's attempt to improve plant production by controlling the environment.

One of the earliest known greenhouses was built somewhere around 30 A.D. for the Roman Emperor Tiberius. Glass had not been invented and the greenhouse, then called a *specularium,* was painstakingly fabricated from small transluscent sheets of mica. All this just to satisfy the Emperor's craving for cucumbers out of season.

Tiberius's greenhouse hardly created a new rage. Aside from the expense, the technology of the greenhouse took centuries to evolve.

It was not until 1599 that the first practical greenhouse was built. Designed by French botanist Jules Charles and constructed in Leiden, Holland, it was intended to grow tropical plants only for medicinal purposes. One of the favorite plants of the day was the tamarind (or Indian date) which Charles had brought back from India.

The greenhouse idea caught on and began spreading throughout Europe. The French, who had a passion for that wonderful new fruit, the orange, began setting up structures to protect their trees from frost. They were, naturally enough, called *orangeries.* But they were cumbersome, as was the one built by Solomon de Caus in Heidelberg around 1619. It had removable shutters on the roof which had to be taken down and put up daily during the frost season. This was no small chore considering that 340 orange trees were under the roof. Indeed, George Washington, perhaps the richest American of his day, craved pineapples, and ordered a greenhouse *pinery* built at Mount Vernon so he could serve pineapples to his guests.

Experiments to improve the greenhouse concept, includ-

ing angled glass walls and heating flues, continued throughout the 17th century. New building technology and better glass led inexorably toward larger and larger greenhouses that housed plants just to please the eyes and palates of European royalty.

The palace of Versailles was an example of the elaborate efforts of the aristocracy to build larger and more spectacular orangeries. The Versailles orangery was more than 500 feet long, 42 feet wide and 45 feet high, with south-facing windows for light and heat.

In Russia, Czar Alexander I was not to be outdone. Between 1801 and 1805, he had built at St. Petersburg three parallel greenhouses, each 700 feet long and connected on each end by two more greenhouses of the same length. Some sections for the tropical plants and fruits were 40 feet high. The entire structure was heated during the bitter Russian winters by furnaces filled with birch wood.

As elaborate as these were, it was the Victorian Age in England that ushered in the golden era of the greenhouse. By the mid-1800s, glass was being manufactured in great quantity and the prohibitive taxes on it were repealed. The wealthy immediately began competing with each other to build the most elaborate greenhouse, again primarily just to house citrus fruits and rare flowers. Little thought was given to using them for a complete range of food production.

The soaring conservatory at Kew Gardens in England is a prime example of the Victorian greenhouse. Its replica, the Conservatory of Flowers, can be seen in San Francisco's Golden Gate Park.

In America, the first greenhouse on record was built around 1737 by Andrew Faneuil, a wealthy Boston merchant. Like his European predecessors, Faneuil used it primarily to grow fruit. The concept spread slowly since almost all greenhouses were built for the wealthy.

By 1825, however, greenhouses were increasingly common. Many were heated by furnace-warmed air. But some of the earliest were pit greenhouses heated largely by sunlight flowing in south-facing windows. This is a design that remains highly practical today.

Indeed, the modern concept of the greenhouse is simple and practical. No longer is it the private domain of the monied class but something that anyone can have for relatively little cost.

Greenhouses today go virtually anywhere there is space, from a window, to a balcony, to a little backyard, or over several acres.

Greenhouse routines are now increasingly automated to reduce the amount of time and care owners must spend. Home production of all kinds of vegetables and flowers is easy. A greenhouse is often attached to the home and used as a solar heat trap to cut heating costs. Going even further, new designs have house and greenhouse totally incorporated. Suddenly there is a biosphere, a living, growing environment where persons and plants can thrive together.

Today a wide variety of public and private greenhouses is in use. Opposite left, Oyster Bay, New York; left, Bailey Arboretum, Locust Valley, New York; above, Conservatory of Flowers, San Francisco, California; above right, Zurich, Switzerland; right, Long Island, New York.

Getting Started

How to evalulate sizes, styles, construction procedures and maintenance costs. How to lay out the site, build foundations and design the interiors.

Greenhouses have come a long way since the wealthy in both Europe and America used them to force oranges and pineapples in so-called *orangeries* and *pineries*. The conservatory developed into a status symbol half way through the past century as well as a practical way for nurserymen to produce almost any crop or plant indoors. Our modern greenhouses are modeled more after the efficient commercial rather than the more beautiful conservatory types of the past century. Now there are dozens of styles to choose from and a wide range of prices. Then, too, home gardeners are discovering they can build their own at a fraction of the cost of buying a greenhouse.

Even if you are a completely inexperienced builder, consider putting up your own greenhouse. There are several different styles of varying complexity in this book for you to consider. Apart from saving money if you build your own, there is the great satisfaction of having done it yourself. In addition, you can make changes as you go along, which is a common trait among all builders.

Greenhouses have proven themselves to be remarkably adaptable to any situation. Instead of the traditional greenhouse simply plunked down somewhere in the backyard, we now see them on rooftops or enclosing sunny balconies on houses and apartments. More and more people are discovering the benefits of making them an extension of the house for people, birds and plants to enjoy.

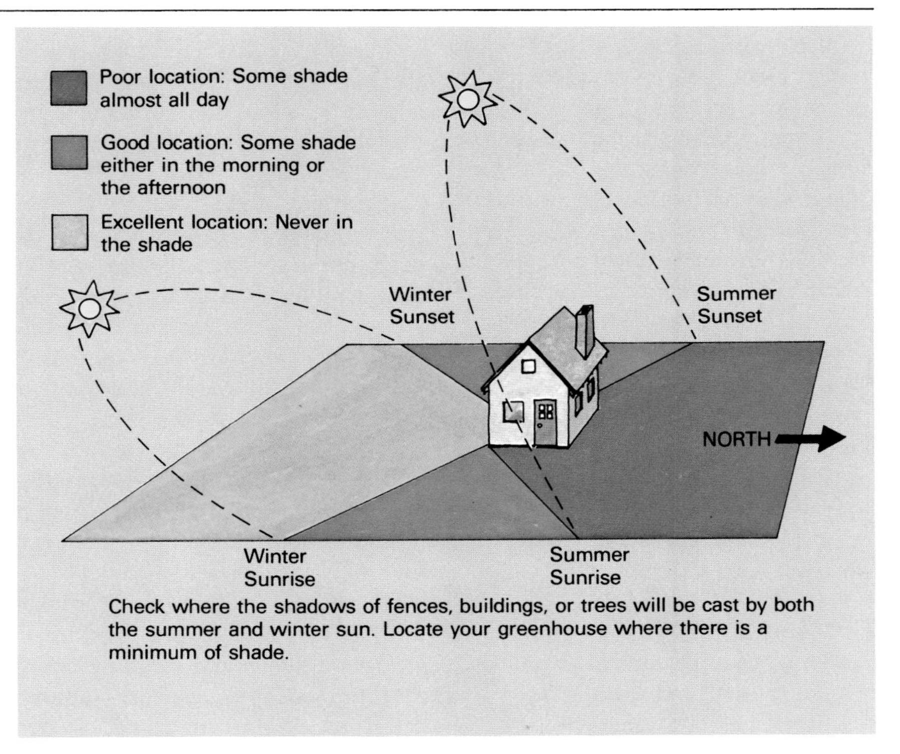

Check where the shadows of fences, buildings, or trees will be cast by both the summer and winter sun. Locate your greenhouse where there is a minimum of shade.

First Considerations
Before you actually buy your greenhouse materials, ask yourself some serious questions.

■ How big a greenhouse do I need? How big a greenhouse can I afford? The answer from greenhouse growers around the country is: make it larger than you anticipate using because once you start greenhouse gardening you will want to expand.

■ Do I want a prefab or do I want to build my own? That consideration includes your available time and money, and just what you want the greenhouse to do. If you would like to build your own but consider yourself too much a novice, hire an experienced carpenter to help you, or consider a prefab type requiring only assembly.

■ Am I supposed to get a building permit? Will a greenhouse result in higher taxes on my property? Happily, many states are enacting laws to give tax rebates on solar heating devices, and you should see if your model of greenhouse can qualify.

■ Are there local design ordinances covering any buildings on residential property where I live? The building permit office can advise you on that. For a building permit—which you'll probably need, whether you have a prefab or are constructing your own—a simple sketch showing the dimensions and supports is usually all that is required.

■ Finally, are there setback requirements for my property? In most residential areas, all buildings have to be set back a certain distance from property lines. Check this point so you won't have to move the greenhouse later.

The prospective greenhouse owner should consider other factors:

■ **Maintenance costs:** How much will you have to pay to maintain the greenhouse and supply it with water and electric light? Can you sell any of your flowers or plants to help offset these costs?

■ **Heating costs:** Whether by electricity, oil or gas, the rates seem to be going up every year. The better your greenhouse is constructed, the less the heat loss. A layer of plastic sheeting inside to create a thermal barrier can cut heat losses up to 40 percent. Using simple solar heating advances can, in some cases, not only eliminate all costs of heating the greenhouse but sharply reduce your residential bill.

■ **Taxes:** Ask either the building permit office or the tax office if your style of greenhouse will be classified as temporary. If so, you may not have to pay additional taxes, or only low ones. If you're really lucky, you may not even need a permit.

Choosing the Site

Deciding where to put that greenhouse is a critical first step. Once it is up, it's there to stay unless you are prepared to go to a lot of expense and effort to move it.

The first consideration is sunshine. Look at your property with a different eye. Is that wall or tree out there going to put too much shade on the greenhouse? Remember also that in the winter the sun will be considerably lower than in the summer. As a rule of thumb, locate the greenhouse a distance away that is 2.5 times the height of a wall or house that might block sunlight.

Is that tree a deciduous one? If so, it can provide shade during part of the hot summer days but allow sunlight in the winter when it drops its leaves.

Drainage is the next consideration. Don't build in depressions that will be catch basins for rain and snow during the winter months. Don't build in boggy areas where the soil is constantly wet and unstable.

Select a site that is relatively level or that can be made level easily. If there is a slope behind the greenhouse, you may have to put in tile or gravel ditches to divert runoff.

Now look at the ground where you want to build. If you expect to plant directly in the soil, then the earth is a big consideration. If it is too rocky or has too much clay, you may have to create new growing beds. It should also drain well so you don't trap water or turn packed earth into mud.

Water and electricity are also two important considerations. The farther the greenhouse is from these connections, the more work it is for you to run the utility lines there.

Consider, too, the trouble it takes for you to walk to your greenhouse in freezing cold and blinding snow. Something close to the house—or even better, attached to the house—is easy to tend during cold winter months. The most important consideration of all is to maximize the winter sunlight.

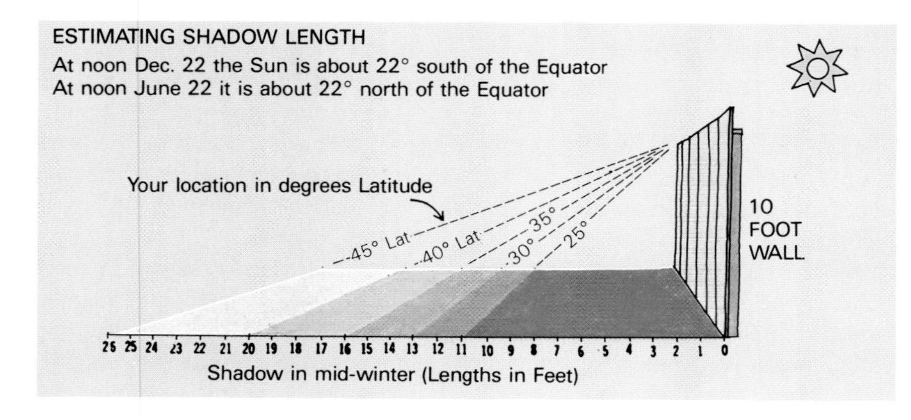

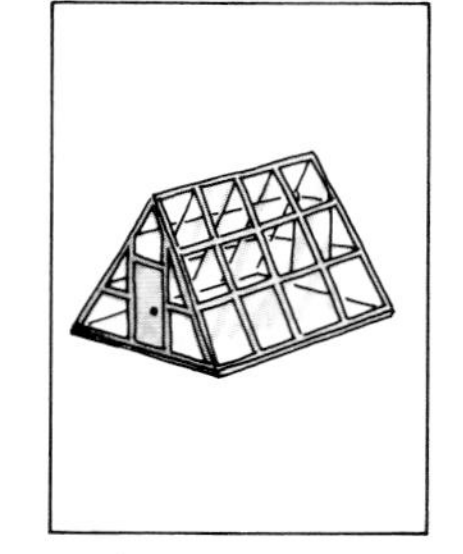

A-frame

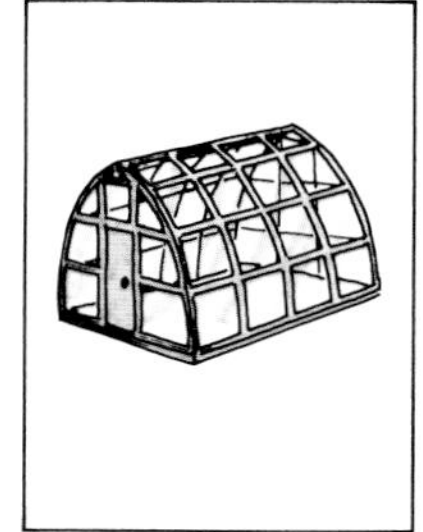

Gothic

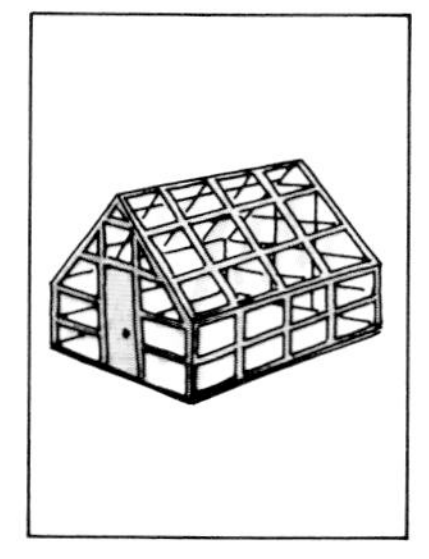

Free-standing

Attached

What Style of Greenhouse?

There are a wide variety of greenhouses you can build yourself and the style you choose will depend on such things as how permanent you want it to be, whether it is attached to the house or freestanding, and what type of snow loads exist in your part of the country.

A-Frame: This can be built in sections on the ground and then raised into place and covered. It is quick to construct. In areas with heavy snow loads, this shape is ideal. However, there is limited head room and proper ventilation is difficult to achieve.

Gothic: The gothic roof line is made from laminated wood strips. With wood, permanent coverings such as corrugated fiberglass can be readily installed.

Free-standing: This is what usually comes to mind when we think of the greenhouse: the conventional glazed building out in the yard. It can be built to any size and covered with anything from glass to polyethylene.

Attached: The attached greenhouse is proving increasingly popular. It can be heated easily from the house but solar heat gained in the greenhouse can be transferred to the main house. Water and electricity are nearby. The greenhouse is within easy reach regardless of the weather outside. It can become a beautiful extension of the house.

Greenhouse Coverings

What you cover the greenhouse with will be influenced by the cost, the ease in putting it up, the permanence desired and your own sense of esthetics.

Glass remains popular because it provides an unobstructed view both into and out of the greenhouse. It can also be very easily shaded when there's too much hot summer sun. Glass is highly resistant to scratching and over the years it can be cleaned repeatedly with no loss in light transmission. Glass is also usually cheaper than the rigid acrylic plastics on the market. The problem with glass is that it breaks and if you live in an area where there are heavy hailstorms, this can be an important consideration. Breakage through vandalism is something else to think about. For roofs, use double-strength glass. Single-strength panes on the walls are sufficient.

Acrylic that is clear and rigid makes superb covering for a greenhouse. It is only about half the weight of glass and ten times more resistant to breakage. It can be easily cut to fit by the home carpenter and even curved for special effects. It allows in 90 to 95 percent of the available light and does not appreciably lose this clarity over 15 or more years of exposure to the suns rays.

Fiberglass covering has proved particularly popular. It comes in both corrugated panels and in flat rolls. They are a boon because of the ease in handling. Simple greenhouses can go up in a day or over a weekend with fiberglass panels. When choosing these panels, ask your building supplier if they are designed for greenhouse use. They must be specially treated (with Tedlar, for example) to prevent the fiberglass from expanding slightly and then trapping dirt, which results in a sharp loss of light transmission. Many greenhouse builders prefer to cover the roof with the corrugated fiberglass panels for their strength and ease in application, and then cover the sides with flat fiberglass or glass.

Polyethylene film is the cheapest covering but also the least durable. It has its advantages where the gardener wants just a temporary covering over a simple greenhouse structure during the winter. It can also be applied over large areas rapidly and at relatively little cost. However, this plastic film, unless treated, can be quickly destroyed by ultraviolet rays. When buying it for greenhouse use, check that it is ultraviolet-resistant.

One of the greatest uses of polyethylene film is as a lining for the inside of greenhouse walls to create a thermal barrier that reduces heat loss.

An attached type greenhouse covered with fiberglass offers simplicity in both design and construction. The panels are lightweight and easy to handle. Seal corrugated fiberglass with styrofoam stripping cut to fit ridges.

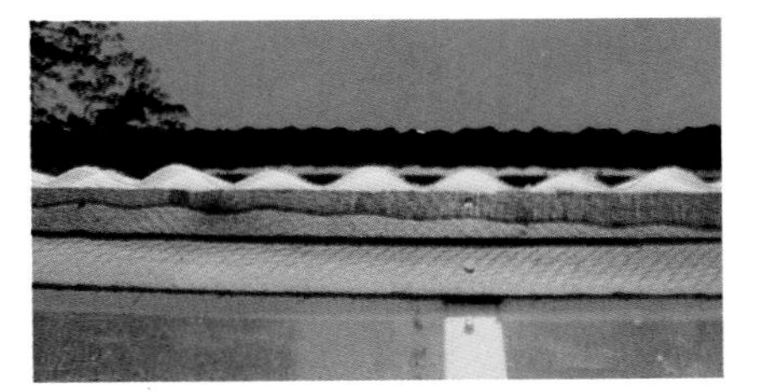

Designs of greenhouses are as varied as their owners. Consider the styles shown above and left as you plan your own. The best design is the one that suits your needs, your location and your gardening interests.

Interior Design

When you are planning the greenhouse, it's vital that you consider what kind of plants you are likely to want to grow. Just as we design our homes for family needs, so should you consider the needs of your plants inside the greenhouse.

Tall plants or vines may require high supports; thus, the A-frame will not be as usable as one of the other styles. Also, consider if you will want to grow in ground beds or entirely on benches or tables.

The bench layout is very important. Remember that benches running north and south get an even distribution of light as the sun moves from east to west. The layout for benches or tables usually follows either the aisle or the peninsula plan. In the first, you simply run two rows of benches end to end, usually along each side of the greenhouse to conserve space, with an aisle between. The peninsula plan, on the other hand, has individual benches running in from the greenhouse sides with very narrow aisles between and a wider aisle down the center. If the greenhouse is big enough, the peninsula plan is probably more satisfactory because there's room in the center aisle to keep plants brought indoors for the winter. But whichever system you choose, remember that it costs as much to heat aisle space as it does the space where the plants grow. You should therefore try to plan a layout that allows no more than a quarter of the total floor space for aisles.

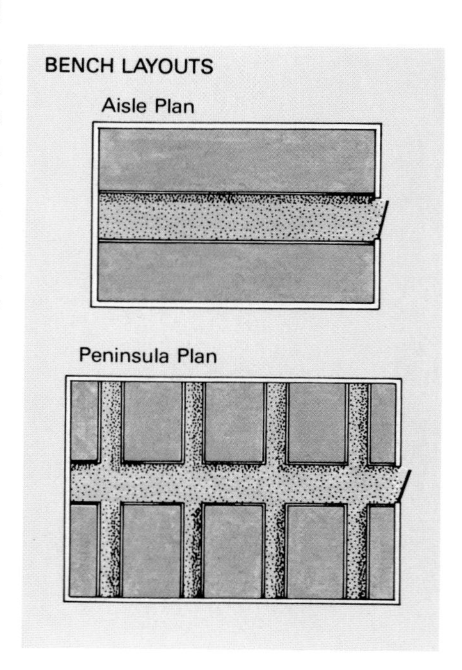

Site Layout and Foundation

After you have decided what type of greenhouse is right for you, and how big it will be, then roll up your sleeves and prepare to work. The first chore, and perhaps the most important, is putting down a foundation that is both level and square. It is a time-consuming and frustrating exercise, especially when you want to see those greenhouse walls go up and flowers bloom. But take your time with the foundation; it will make life much easier for you later on. There's nothing quite as frustrating as walls and roofs that don't fit because the foundation isn't square.

Now, there are foundations and there are foundations. Unless you are an experienced builder, in which case you wouldn't have to read this, these directions are confusing. There are new terms and concepts for you to deal with. If you do have an experienced builder to assist you, these ideas will quickly become clear. Otherwise, read and reread and follow the drawings and photographs. Once you begin, everything will start to fall into place. Remember, people who build skyscrapers, at some point in time knew no more about building than you do now.

This section deals essentially with the traditional concrete footing and how to pour it level and square. But many people want only a simple and lightly-framed greenhouse, with a plastic or fiberglass covering, that does not require an extensive foundation. For those structures, go ahead and use a light foundation. It can be made by simply laying out painted railroad ties that are either sunk in ditches to just above ground level or staked with iron reinforcing rods (also called "rerod bars" or "rebars").

Another easy foundation (in mild climate areas) starts with a 6-inch deep ditch dug to the size of your greenhouse, then lined with concrete building blocks that you fill with cement. Insert some anchor bolts for your frame and you're set to build. Or you can sink precast concrete piers every four feet around the perimeter and build up from there.

Whatever you choose for a foundation, it must be level and square. So the best thing for us to do is to start there.

Laying It Out

The site for the greenhouse should be level, or almost so. First to go in will be the footing, which is normally concrete and should go at least 8 inches below the surface of the ground, or deeper, if necessary, to get below the frost line. If you put the footing too shallow, the ground below may freeze and heave, cracking both the footing and your greenhouse.

On top of the footing goes the foundation wall and on top of that goes the framework for the greenhouse. The rule of thumb is that the footing should be twice the width of the foundation. Thus, if you plan to make the foundation wall of the standard 8-inch concrete blocks, the footing will be 16 inches wide.

Let's assume the foundation wall will be 2 feet high. To start, drive a 2×2 stake firmly in the ground at one corner, leaving 2 feet of the stake above ground. This is point A. Measure off another corner and drive a stake there. This is point B. This is one side of the building and all the other angles to it must be square. Drive a small nail in the top center of each stake and connect them with a tightly drawn string.

To put in the next point, C, measure the distance and use a carpenter's square to make it as close to a 90° angle as you can. Drive a temporary stake in at point C and connect B and C with string.

Now you must make sure that the AB and BC strings form an exact 90° angle. From point B toward point A, measure exactly 8 feet and mark it on the string with a felt pen. Now, from B toward C, measure off exactly 6 feet and mark that point. For the corner B to be square, there must be exactly 10 feet between the marks on the two strings. So with a friend or two helping, adjust the stake at point C until you have that 10 feet on the diagonal.

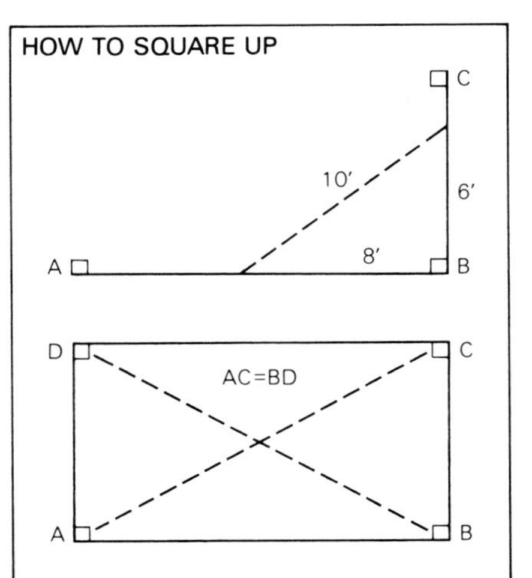

For the third leg, from A to D, measure it as closely as you can, then drive a temporary stake at corner D. Make sure the distance from A to D is the same as from B to C. Using the same trick of marking the strings at 6 and 8 foot, adjust until square.

Now for the final proof that everything is square: measure both the diagonals, from A to C and from B to D. If they are the same, everything is square. Allowing for slack in the measuring tape and difficulty in measuring the string, a difference of ⅛ inch for a small structure or ¼ inch for a large one is allowable. But, if the difference in your diagonals is larger, you had better go over the measurements again.

Batter Boards

The stakes and string you just put up show the exact outside measurements of the greenhouse. The next step is to lay out the footings. For this, batter boards are needed at the four corners. These batter boards will allow you to remove the stakes and strings when you dig the footing trench and still know exactly where the corners are.

Start by driving a 2×4 stake about 2 feet back from the corner stakes and directly on the diagonal from the opposite corner. Drive two more stakes 4 feet from the corner down each side of the building outline to form a right angle. Check with a large square. These stakes should be about 2 feet above the ground and must be level. Connect with 1×4 boards nailed flush with the top of the stakes. Use a level to check the boards.

Now construct batter boards at the three remaining corners in the same fashion. These batter boards must all be on the same level. If you don't have a small hand transit to check, stretch string tightly and check with a line level.

Now pull another set of strings directly over the four building outline strings and make small saw cuts in the

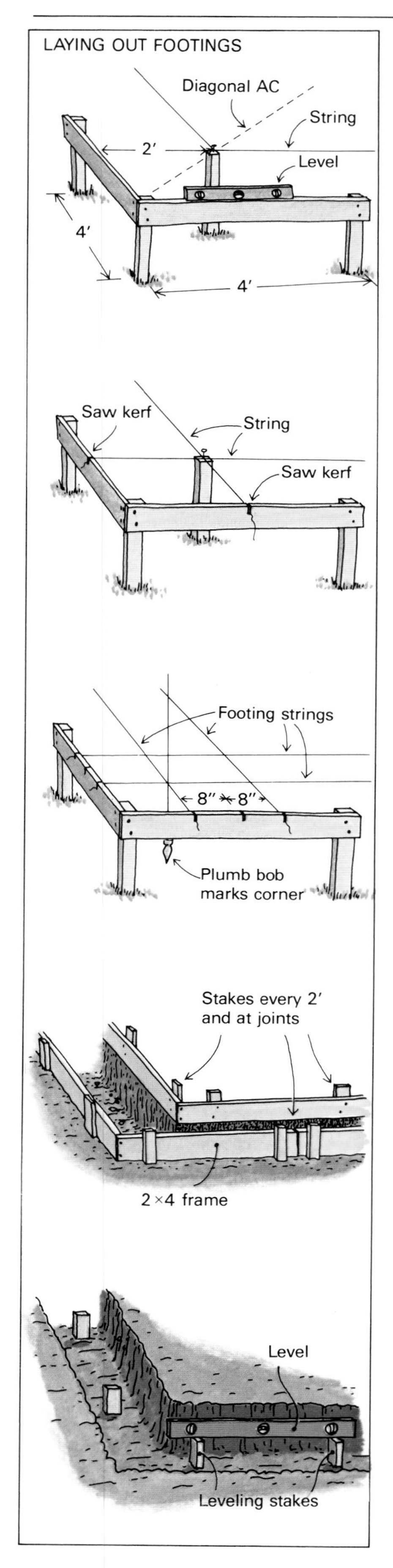

batter board to mark their line. Make the building outline in string pulled tightly through the saw cuts on the batter boards. Remove the original stakes and string and also remove the string from the batter boards. Since you have made saw cuts in each batter board where they go, you can put the strings quickly back in place when you need them.

You're ready to mark the outline for the footings. If you are going to build up a concrete block wall, the footing should technically be 16 inches wide, or twice that of the standard 8-inch wide concrete block. If you are not going to have a foundation wall but want to put the greenhouse directly on the footings, 12 inches wide will be ample. Check with the building codes for the final word, however.

For a 16-inch footing, mark off 8 inches on each side of the saw kerf in the batter boards and pull strings all around. Using a plumb bob, drive small stakes at the inside and outside points for each corner. Now snap a chalk line on the ground to mark the footing outline and then remove the strings.

For a footing that will be 8 inches deep and will have a foundation wall on top, make the trench 10 inches deep. This will keep the footings 2 inches below ground and out of sight.

If, however, you plan to build directly on the footing, then you should bring it up above ground a few inches to keep the greenhouse walls clear of the ground. Do this by nailing together a 2×4 frame flush with the edges of the footing trench, inside and outside. Stake it every 2 feet for added strength since concrete is heavy and can easily bow out weak frames. This frame must be level all the way around before you pour.

For a footing that will remain 2 inches below the ground level, the big question is how to make it level when you pour the concrete. The sides of the trench are too inaccurate for this purpose. The answer is leveling stakes. For a footing 8 inches deep, start in the center of the trench at one corner and drive a 2×2 stake firmly in the ground with exactly 8 inches showing. Now proceed around the trench, driving stakes every 4 to 7 feet with just 8 inches showing. Use a straight 2×4 stud and a carpenter's level to check each one. When you return to the original stake, you must still be on the same level. Now, when you pour exactly to the top of the stakes, you know your footing will be level. Don't worry about removing these stakes: just let them stay in the concrete. But before you pour the concrete, plan your water and electricity hookups as described later.

Ready To Pour

Before pouring, line the bottom of the trench with large rocks. The concrete will bind tightly around them and the rocks mean less concrete you have to pour. Some codes may require you to lay concrete reinforcing rods, called rerods or rebar, but this is not customary.

In a wheelbarrow, if you don't have a mixer, combine one shovel of Portland cement, two shovels of sand and four shovels of gravel. Mix thoroughly while dry and then slowly add water. Keep mixing and be careful that all the mix gets wet. From this point it takes only a little more water until you have a mix that is completely wet and loose without being runny.

After you have filled the footing trench to what appears to be the proper level, take a troweling tool and work the mix vigorously until all the air bubbles are out and the mix has settled. You may then have to add some more. Work this again until all the gravel is below the surface and you have a smooth, level top ready for the foundation blocks. Use a concrete "float" for the final smoothing.

When you are ready to pour, you can order a truckload of mixed concrete.

If you're going to build directly onto the footings, insert the anchor bolts now. Leave 2½ inches of the threaded end exposed and make sure they are perpendicular by checking with a square.

Keep the footings covered at night with plastic or straw or both if you are in an area where it is freezing. It will take at least three days for the footings to set enough for you to start the foundation wall. Lightly sprinkle the concrete with water on the second and third day to prevent too rapid drying which will cause it to crack.

Walls

The foundation or side wall for a greenhouse can be both attractive and functional. This wall, usually 24 to 30 inches high, is not high enough to shade much in the greenhouse but it keeps rain and snow from wetting your greenhouse sill.

Before you start the wall, you need to find the exact outline and corners again. Put the string back in the saw kerfs you made in the batter boards and pull it tight all the way around. To mark the corners, hang a plumb bob from the point where each string crosses. Next, use a chalk marker to snap lines from corner to corner on the footing.

The walls are usually made from concrete blocks that are 16 inches long, 8 inches high and 8 inches wide. (Actually, all measurements are just ⅜ inch less so that you can lay ⅜ inch of mortar to bond the blocks.)

Start at one corner and lay that first block very precisely. The rest of the wall will be determined by how square and level that first block is.

Use a mortar mix that is one part mortar cement (not Portland) to four parts of fine sand. Mix dry and then add water until it is smooth and plastic, not runny. Trowel the mortar across the predampened footing and place the first block. Check that it is level and square. Note that corner blocks have one flat end for facing while the others have two grooved ends for joining. You get a mixture when you order blocks.

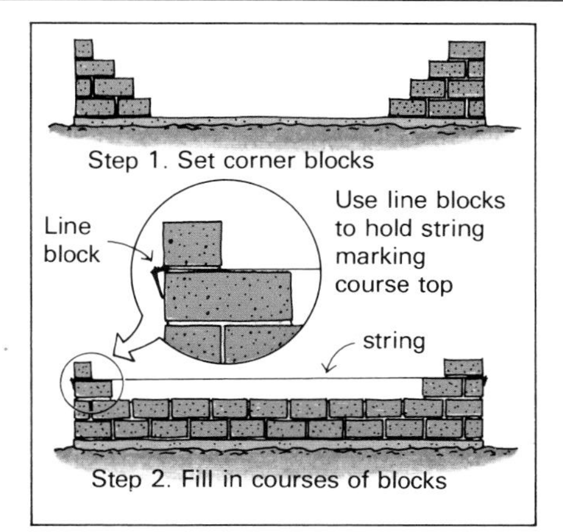

Lay up the four corners first, extending the bottom layer enough each time to support the next layer at the corners.

To join the blocks, stand one on end and "butter" the exposed end with ⅜ to ½ inch of mortar, then fit it to the adjoining block. To join stacking blocks, butter the top of a block on the inside and outside edges, then lay the next block on top of it. It is not customary to butter the cross groove but you should note that one end of it is wide and the other is narrow. The wide end always goes up so you can apply mortar to it.

After the corners are up to the desired height, start laying the rest of the courses. To keep these level, use line blocks that hook over the ends of the blocks with a string stretched tightly between. You can also put perpendicular poles at each corner with marks every 8 inches for the strings.

Blocks also come in half sizes and you will want to order a quantity with the initial order. They are needed on corners and they sometimes fit in the middle of the course. The more common case is that you have to cut a block to fit. Allow ½ inch on each end for the mortar and then cut the block by first scoring all around with a cold chisel and then snapping it apart with the chisel and hammer. Wear safety goggles for this.

There are also special blocks recessed to accept door jambs, which you will need for framing the door openings.

Greenhouse foundation walls only shade below the benches. They help protect the sill from adverse weather and reduce heat loss.

Building the Greenhouse

From attached greenhouses to free-standing gambrels, and A-frames to gothic arches, here is a variety of plans on how to build your own.

When the foundation is finished you have reached a milestone in the construction of your greenhouse. You are well on your way to being able to plant and grow your first crop.

This is also the time to make the final decision on the shape the house will take. If you have a special plan, such as a hemispherical dome or an attached greenhouse, this decision will have had to have been made before you laid the foundation. But if you have a basic rectangular foundation, with or without a wall, there is still time to reconsider ideas you may have had while you worked on that foundation. Review again the basic shapes you could use:

The A-Frame—easy to build, ideal for areas with heavy snow loads, but head room is limited and good ventilation is difficult to achieve.

The Gothic Arch—lovely to look at but a challenging project for the home craftsman because the layout and lamination of the arches takes time.

The Free-standing Even Span Gable—a free-standing greenhouse that is probably the most typical and usable shape to build: the interior space layout is very practical and there's easy access for a loaded wheelbarrow through a door at either end.

The Attached—easy access from house with water and electricity nearby.

After you have made your final decision on the greenhouse shape and ordered the material, you are ready to move ahead.

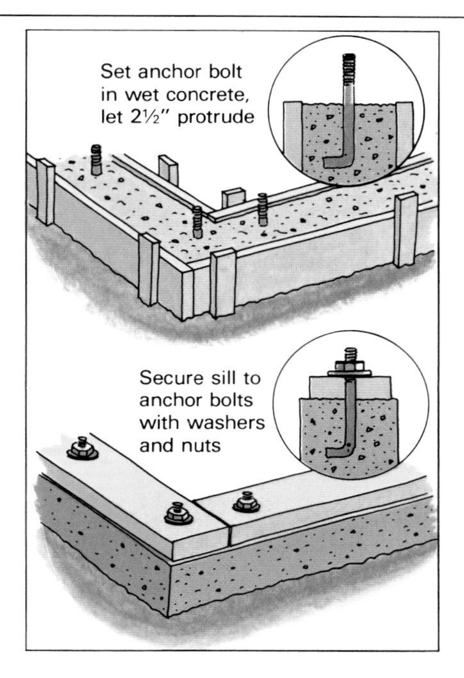

The Sill

The sill is a board—preferably 2×6 redwood—that goes flat around the top of the footing or foundation wall and gives you something to nail to when you put up the greenhouse walls. The sill is bolted to the foundation with anchor bolts. Space them 4 to 6 feet apart, always putting one near the ends of each length of sill. Measure so that a bolt doesn't come where a stud will stand.

If you have a concrete block wall, hold the concrete in place by pushing wads of paper down each opening where the anchor bolt will go. Fill the top of the opening with concrete and anchor the bolt vertically in place. Leave 2½ inches exposed.

When the concrete has set, place lengths of 2×6 redwood exactly in line over the foundation and then tap the sill with a hammer above each anchor bolt. Drill these guide marks out. When the sill is bolted in place all around, you're ready to start putting up walls. We describe that exercise later for the different styles of greenhouse.

Water Lines

It is best to run the water lines to the greenhouse entirely underground. This way they won't freeze in the winter and there will be no unsightly pipes showing.

The pipes can be laid in a trench that runs under the footing before you pour. You don't have to fully install the water lines: under the footing just lay in a section of plastic pipe (PVC) that you can connect later. If you forget or already have a greenhouse foundation, you can dig down and then shove the PVC pipe through, since it is quite flexible.

If you want to put water pipes through a concrete block wall, first score the block with a circle slightly larger than the pipe. Tap it out with a cold chisel and run the pipe through. Use a mortar mix to fill the hole around the pipe.

The only complications in hooking up water lines come in tying into your main supply line. Whether you do this outside or have to go under the house, the easiest water pipe material to work with is PVC. The plastic cuts easily and glues together in seconds. It is also flexible which makes it easier for you to go around curves or under footings.

If you are in an area with little or no freezing and you want only a cold water tap in the greenhouse, the easiest way to get water is to hook into an outside spiggot. However, in the end, the easiest way may not be the best, because the exposed line may freeze up.

If you do decide to run cold water from an outside spigot, the first step is to check the pipe carefully to see what size it is, and whether it has male or female fittings. Then make your purchases. Now, with the water shut off, attach a T-fitting and screw the spigot back on one side.

Your greenhouse line will come from the other side. The line can be as small as ½-inch if you don't have a long distance to move the water. A ¾-inch line would give you more water and would probably be more practical. If you have to carry the water 100 feet or more, go to a 1-inch line.

To hook up the greenhouse water line, first screw a PVC bushing onto the T-fitting. Glue a short length of pipe into that and then add a 90° elbow that points straight down. From this elbow you can run a line down into the ground and over to your greenhouse. Install a PVC gate just above the ground. This will allow you to shut off the water to the greenhouse should the line spring a leak at some time.

If you want hot water in the greenhouse, you are going to have to tie into the hot water heater supply lines in your house. In many cases these are copper pipes. These can be connected to PVC water lines but first you must install a copper T-joint in the pipes. To do this requires a moderate skill in using a propane torch and solder to "sweat" the fittings.

However, if you take your water pipe plans to a plumbing shop, they will give you all the necessary fittings and perhaps a little more. If you buy the materials required for sweating copper joints at that store, and come in when the manager is not busy, it's likely he will show you how to do the job yourself.

PVC Pipe

PVC pipe comes in a variety of sizes and strengths to withstand different water pressures. For home use, you will want "Schedule 40" which is more than adequate for residential water pressures. The pipe can be cut with a hacksaw or a regular crosscut saw. After it's cut, smooth the inside burred edge with a pocket knife or rough sand paper. Before gluing, sand the outside of the pipe and the inside of the coupling to roughen the surface. When you glue, apply a moderate coat to both the pipe and the coupling. Put them together and give a quarter-turn twist. When putting on an angle coupling, make sure you twist it exactly into place the first time. The special PVC glue sets in seconds so be careful not to make any alignment mistakes.

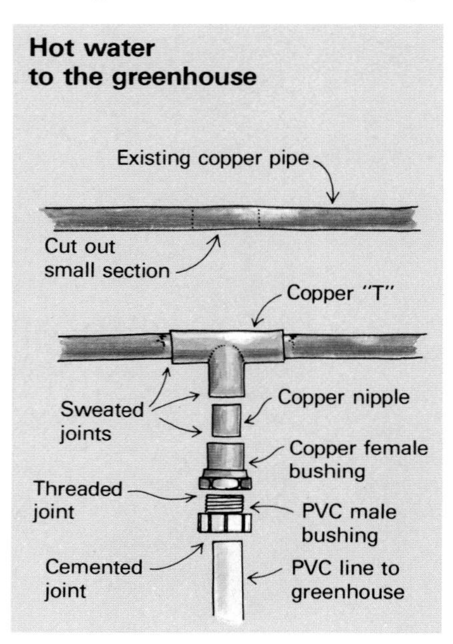

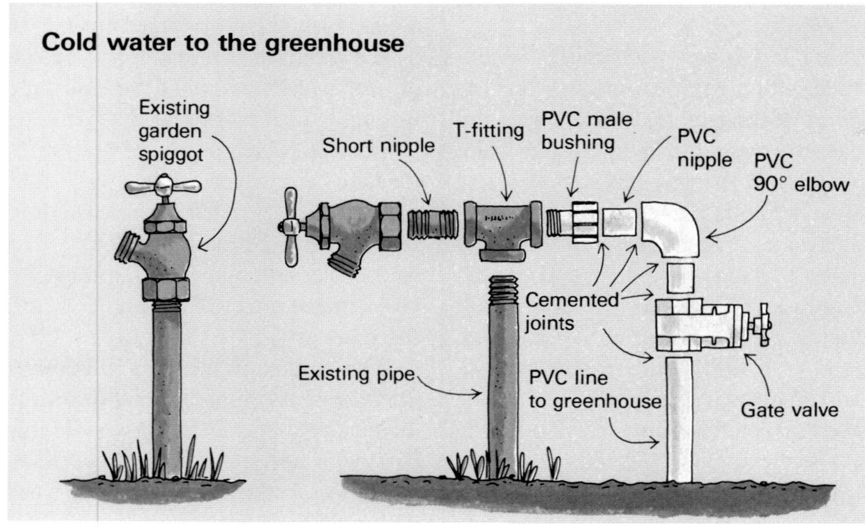

Electric Connections

Unless you are experienced in working with electricity, this phase of your greenhouse will require an expert. An electrician's knowledge is needed in determining how much electricity will be required in your greenhouse and whether a hookup can be made on your existing panel or whether a separate meter and panel is needed. Remember that heat cables for propagation beds, extra lights and fans take careful figuring. All operating at once, they draw considerable power. Make sure you get help before you start.

You can save yourself considerable expense by doing all the groundwork before the electrician gets there. Check with the building code office for the size of wire needed and then buy that size and the length needed, as well as the necessary plugs. Lay the wire at least 3 feet underground in plastic conduit tubing from the greenhouse to where it will enter the residence. With everything ready, the electrician can complete the hookups in a minimum of time.

A Variety of Plans

Here we present several plans for different kinds of greenhouses, but remember that it is *your* greenhouse designed for *your* style of gardening that you are constructing. Select the plan that comes closest to what you want, then use your own ingenuity—and perhaps advice from an experienced builder — to adapt it to your space and circumstances.

On a sunny day—no matter the outside temperature—a greenhouse will trap considerable heat. In the greenhouse shown above, the temperature is a balmy 80 degrees F.

The Attached Greenhouse

The most practical of all greenhouses is one that becomes a part of your own house. In the first place, it is close during the winter months. Construction is made easier because one wall of the greenhouse is actually your house wall and the structure is better braced this way.

An 8×12 foot lean-to model is the first greenhouse dealt with here because it is among the easiest to put together. Once the foundation is down and all the supplies on hand, two people can easily put it up in a weekend. It is made from 2×4 redwood and fiberglass panels treated for greenhouse use.

This section will take you through some of the minute details in construction—and that means even if you aren't an experienced builder, you can put this greenhouse together. Once you learn these basics you can expand on them or build other styles of greenhouses.

This greenhouse is built against a south-facing wall. The first step is to put in a simple foundation. It is laid out and squared as previously described. Because this greenhouse is so light, a simpler foundation was chosen: precast concrete piers spaced 4 feet apart. When the concrete blocks are put in place, with 2 inches showing, they are tied together with a 2×4 redwood sill. The walls are constructed in units and nailed to this sill. The back wall is a house wall directly under an overhanging eave. A 2×6 ledger board 12 feet long is fastened to the house wall with lag screws sunk into every other stud. The bottom of the ledger board is set at 8 feet high and the front wall at 6 feet in height.

The next step is the front wall. In the greenhouse we built the front wall was 6 feet high and angled back at a 70° slope to catch the winter sun more effectively. This process is described in more detail in the solar greenhouse section. It is not a difficult trick but if this is your first construction experience, it is easier to make the front wall vertical.

For the wall to be 6 feet high, cut the studs 5 feet 9 inches long, which allows 3 inches for the top and bottom plates. The plates are the horizontal members that the side wall studs are attached to at the top and bottom; the rafters lay across them at the top. The plates can be made from 2×4s.

Studs and roof rafters are placed 2 feet on-center and covered with 4-foot wide panels of fiberglass: corrugated on the roof and flat on the sides.

To lay out the wall, put the top and bottom plate side by side flat on the ground or driveway. Mark off every 2 feet on the boards, using a carpenter's square to mark both plates at the same time. One of the legs of your carpenter's square is 1½ inches wide, the same as a 2×4. Lay it directly over the center of the mark and pencil in lines on each side.

Lay out the wall with plates and studs in place and then nail together. Stand on one stud while nailing on the plate to keep the frame from shifting.

Note that the on-center distance between the first stud and the second is only 23¼ inches. The extra ¼ inch will be taken up outside by overlapping one extra ridge when putting on the corrugated fiberglass.

A vent is almost essential in the front wall, as it is in the roof, to prevent overheating during summer months. You can use a jalousie window as we did or build a wood-frame and fiberglass vent.

You're now ready to stand up the first wall. With friends helping, place the wall on the foundation and nail and brace it.

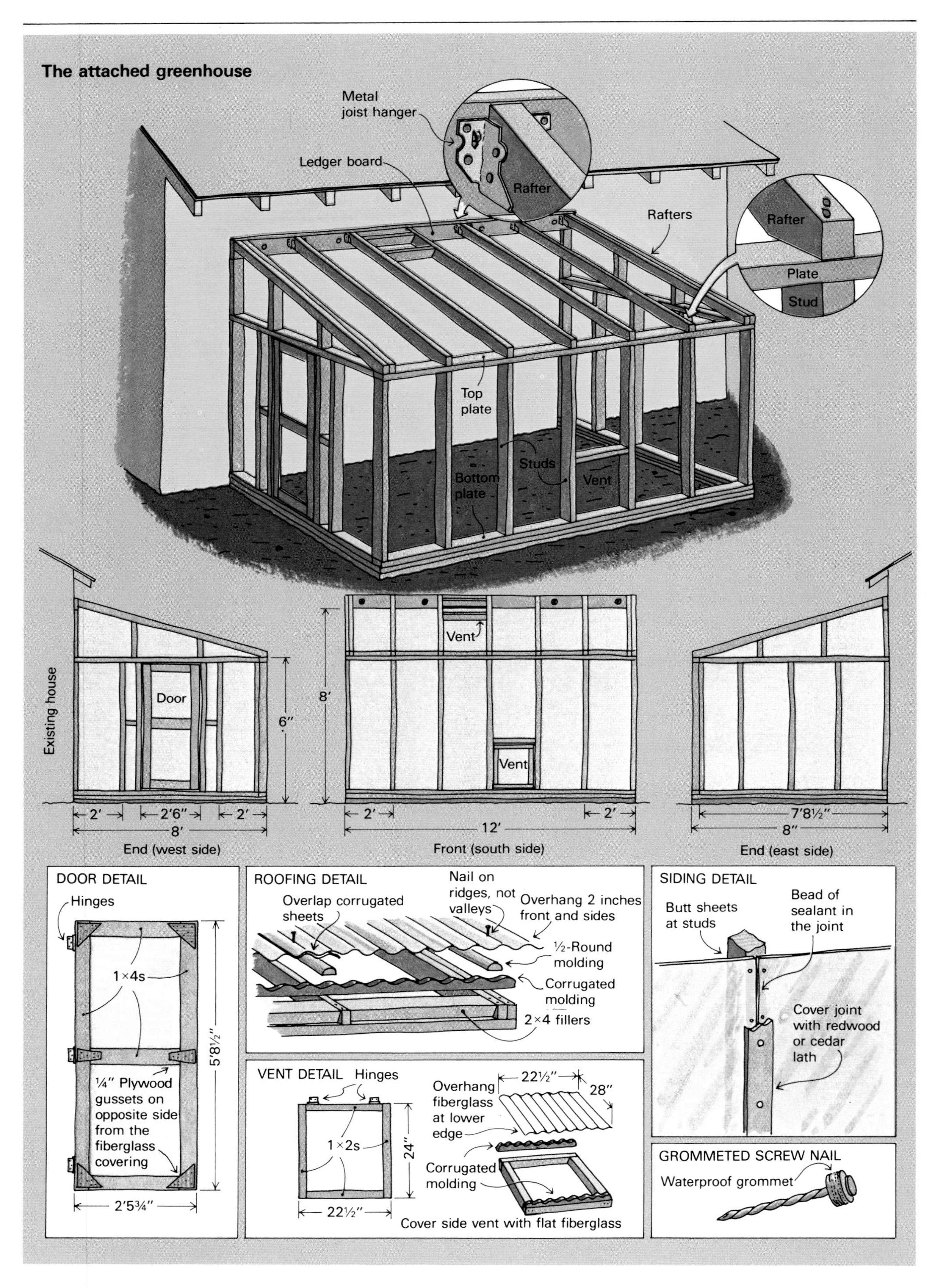
The attached greenhouse
Metal joist hanger
Ledger board
Rafter
Rafters
Rafter
Plate
Stud
Top plate
Studs
Bottom plate
Vent
Existing house
Door
6"
8'
Vent
Vent
2'
2'6"
2'
8'
End (west side)
2'
2'
12'
Front (south side)
7'8½"
8"
End (east side)
DOOR DETAIL
Hinges
1×4s
¼" Plywood gussets on opposite side from the fiberglass covering
5'8½"
2'5¾"
ROOFING DETAIL
Overlap corrugated sheets
Nail on ridges, not valleys
Overhang 2 inches front and sides
½-Round molding
Corrugated molding
2×4 fillers
VENT DETAIL
Hinges
1×2s
24"
22½"
Overhang fiberglass at lower edge
22½"
28"
Corrugated molding
Cover side vent with flat fiberglass
SIDING DETAIL
Butt sheets at studs
Bead of sealant in the joint
Cover joint with redwood or cedar lath
GROMMETED SCREW NAIL
Waterproof grommet

Now you're ready to attach the side walls. These go up essentially as the front wall did.

Allowing for the 3½ inch width of the end studs on the front wall, the plates on the 8-foot end walls will be 7 feet 8½ inches long. The studs for the end walls will be 5 feet 9 inches, the same as the front wall and again 2 feet on-center. Cut, mark, and assemble the end wall without the door the same way you did the front wall.

For the end wall with the door, mark and constuct it essentially the same except leave a space in the center for the width of your 30-inch door plus ¼ inch. Frame it with studs and then nail in cross braces on each side to keep the wall from shivering every time you close the door.

Note that the door on this plan is only 5 feet 9 inches high — you may have to duck a little to go through. If it's important for you to have a taller door, refer to the alternate, more difficult to construct, end wall plan that will accommodate a standard 30 inch by 80 inch door.

Nail the end walls into place as you did the front wall. Again double check that they are vertical.

With both end walls in place, you're ready to raise the roof. The roof will consist of 2×4 rafters, 2 feet on-center, that will line up with the studs in the front wall. They will be attached to the ledger board on the back wall with metal joist hangers and nailed to the top plate of the front wall.

Start by putting an uncut 2×4 rafter in place and mark how it must be cut to fit in the joist hanger and angle down to the wall. With the rafter held against the end of the plate, mark with a pencil the angle of the cut so it will lie flush on top of the plate. When that rafter is cut and rechecked, use it as a pattern to cut the other rafters. Note that if you have a vertical front wall 8 feet out from your house, you will have to buy the standard 10 foot lengths of 2×4 and cut them to fit. At each end of the roof, put two 2×4 rafters together to make a 4×4. This makes it easy for you to nail in the vertical pieces that fill in the angle between the top plate on the wall and the rafters. These pieces are not needed for support, only for something on which to nail the covering. Put one against the house wall between the top plate and ledger board and one or two others as you see fit.

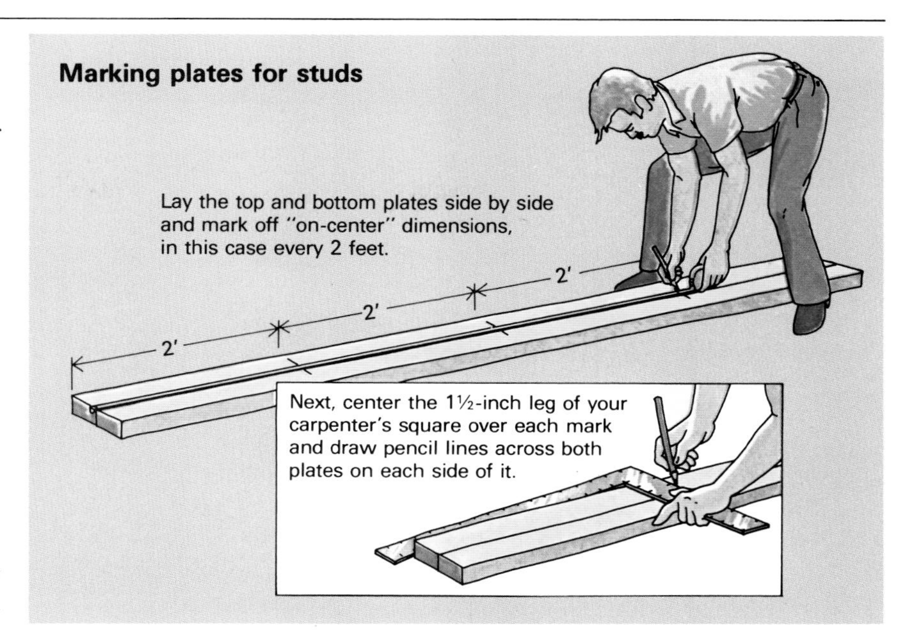

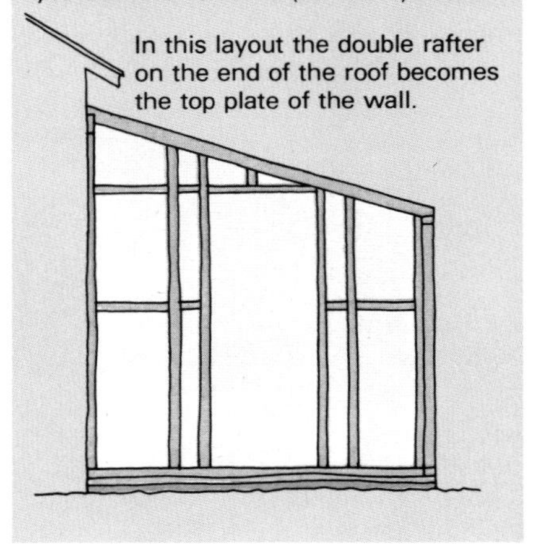

Next cut short lengths of 2 × 4s to fill in between the rafters. Nail the wide part of the 2×4 flush with the top of the rafters just at the front edge.

Vents

The vents here are essentially frames to hold pieces of fiberglass that fit in between the studs or rafters. Here we describe the construction of the roof vent. The vent in the front wall is built the same way, but covered with flat fiberglass to match the wall.

Start by making a frame of 2×2s that is 24 inches long and 22½ inches wide, just able to fit between the studs or rafters. Tack redwood corrugated molding, or rubber molding, on the top and bottom widths and attach a 28-inch length of fiberglass roofing. The 4-inch overhang in front assures no leaks.

You cannot nail through the panels without breaking them. Lay them in place and drill holes with a 5/32-inch bit, 12 inches apart down the rafters. Use aluminum nails with neoprene washers to prevent any leaks. Nail every third ridge on cross braces. The nail your hardware man will sell you to attach the fiberglass is called a screw-nail. It has a waterproofing grommet attached and a wide screw thread, but you hammer it in. The nail should always be put through a ridge in the plastic rather than a gutter to prevent leakage. Don't hammer the nail in too far —just so the head and grommet are snug and secure with the plastic.

From the back of the roof frame, where the vent will hinge, measure down 2 feet and put a cross brace. The vent frame should fit smoothly into this opening. With it in place, nail quarter-round molding to the rafters and braces right beneath the frame to support it. After the roofing panels are nailed in place with an allowance for the vent openings, install the vents and hinge them to the back plate. Use a hook and eyebolt fastener to keep them from blowing open.

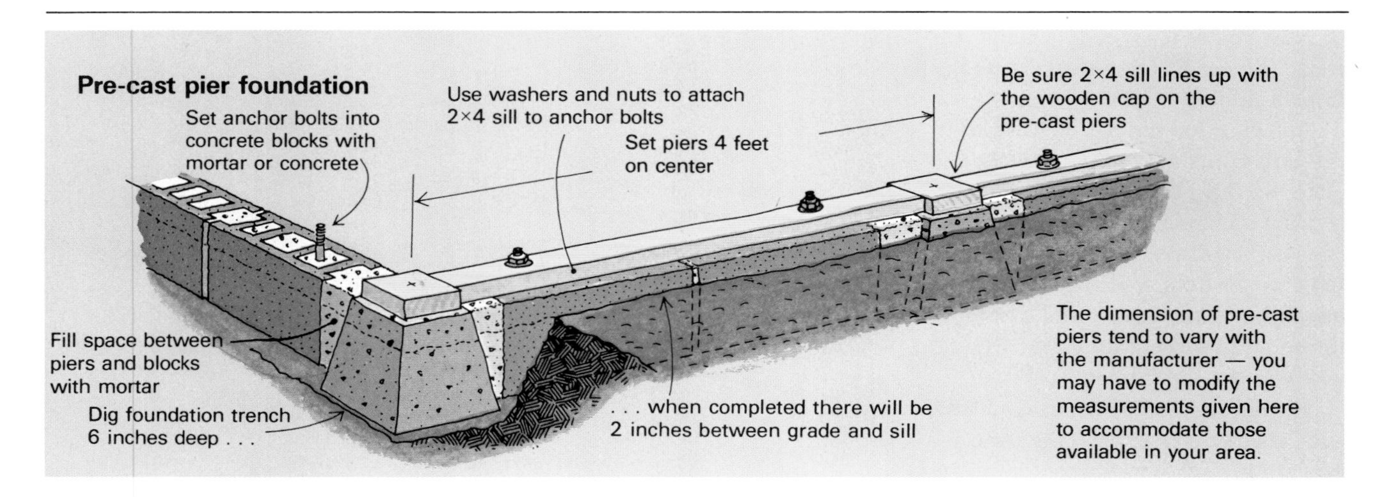

The Roof and Sides

With all the framing done and both vents completed, you are finally ready to complete the roof and walls.

At the top, along the ledger board, and bottom, across the rafters and filler 2×4s, nail on corrugated foam molding. This follows the same waves as the fiberglass panels and prevents drafts. Down each rafter put half-round molding strips to support the corrugated fiberglass. If you use rubber or redwood molding, lay a thin bond of sealant on the molding before you nail the fiberglass panels into place.

Put the panels in place with a 2-inch overhang in front for water runoff. Cut the panels to fit flush with the two vent openings. Across the front, where you may get strong winds trying to pull the roof loose, put a nail in every ridge for extra insurance.

The walls are best covered with flat fiberglass. This makes a tighter fit under the roof line and the flat fiberglass is easier to cut than the corrugated. Measure and cut the front panels first and nail them in place only after you are sure each panel is square. Lay a bead of sealant over each joint and then cover it with strips of redwood lath.

The sides are covered in the same way, with redwood lath holding the panels tightly under the slightly extended roof.

In one greenhouse, we used flat fiberglass for the sides and front. We cut it to size easily with common tin snips. A bead of sealant (available from most greenhouse suppliers) prevents drafts. Roof panels were sealed with foam molding.

The Floor

The easiest way to floor a greenhouse is simply to leave the ground bare and use part of it for planting. The problem with this is that the center walkway generally turns to mud as you water plants and as humidity builds up in the greenhouse. You can counter this by laying natural flagstone, large paving blocks or round concrete pads sold by many garden supply centers.

Many gardeners like to lay down 3 to 4 inches of gravel as a simple but effective floor. It keeps feet out of the mud, it's inexpensive and it's certainly easy to apply. You can water freely in the greenhouse and just let the water run into the gravel where it will help increase humidity.

Some people build on a poured concrete slab but this is both costly and unwise. It means a lot of extra work for you to be mopping and sweeping all the time to keep that floor clean. With other kinds of floors the water and fine dirt takes care of itself by working back into the ground.

One of the most attractive and at the same time practical floors is brick on sand. This works equally well for a small plastic greenhouse or an extension right off your house. In fact, many houses in the Southwest have brick on sand floors in the main house and just extend them when a greenhouse or garden room is added.

In addition to letting water and fine grit disappear through the floor, the bricks will catch and hold solar heat during the day and release it back into the greenhouse at night for added warmth. Black bricks will absorb more heat. Buy 3½ bricks per square foot of floor area.

After you're all done framing and glazing the greenhouse, put down a 3-inch layer of sand. You may have to excavate the floor a little so that by the time you finish with the sand and the bricks your floor is not above the door sill.

An alternative is to place a brick walkway between 2×4s down the center of the greenhouse and spread gravel on the rest of the floor.

Before you start laying the bricks, experiment and see what pattern pleases your eye most. The simplest is the running bond; straight and clean lines. The herringbone and basketweave patterns offer more variety to the eye but are also more difficult to lay. Experiment and come up with your own patterns, perhaps using combinations of brick and patio blocks, or brick and redwood blocks.

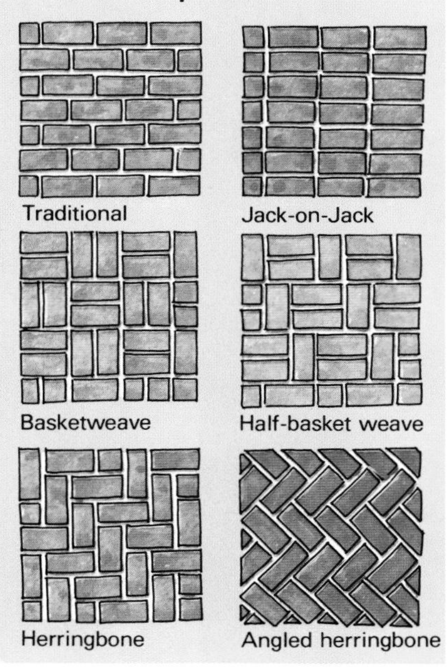

After you put the sand in the greenhouse and spread it around evenly and fairly level, dampen it thoroughly to settle it. Working on a piece of plywood to prevent your knees from digging up the sand, level a section along the back wall with a 2×4. Start laying the bricks in one corner and keep working out from there. If you have benches down only one side, start opposite them so the less finished edge of bricks will be under the benches.

As you lay the brick, always check your level. After you finish a section, lay a 2×4 along a row of bricks and hammer it firmly to set and level the bricks.

Set the bricks as snugly as you can against each other. There will still be about a ⅛-inch gap. These gaps will later be filled in with sand.

Bricks do not break cleanly, which is frustrating when you try to fit them into the leftover spaces against walls. You might want to rent a masonry saw. Otherwise, score the brick first with a cold chisel and then make a single sharp cut. If you feel the edges are too uneven when you're done, hide them by laying down a 2×2 redwood baseboard all around.

After the bricks are in place, cover them with a layer of sand. Leave the layer of sand on the bricks for a couple of days while you walk around. The floor will quickly be as tight and firm as if it had been mortared. Then use a broom to sweep the sand back and forth until all the cracks are filled.

In houses and garden rooms, you can wax the bricks for a finished appearance, but this is not necessary in a greenhouse where you want them to remain porous.

To cut a brick to size, score first, then break with a single sharp stroke with a cold chisel. Cover uneven edges with a 2x2 redwood baseboard. Leave about an ⅛ inch gap between bricks.

A greenhouse gardener admiring her Cattleya orchid in a hanging basket. Amaryllis flowers in the foreground.

This is a typical design for a prefab greenhouse. The frame is redwood; the covering is "Filon" corrugated fiberglass. Cost is low and construction relatively simple.

Greenhouses you can buy

Many potential greenhouse owners don't have the time, tools, or desire to build from scratch. Here we assure them that the range of greenhouses they can purchase is wide.

The two typical variables when deciding how to get a greenhouse are ambition and the budget. Energetic gardeners will get started with a plan from this book or from a slightly less challenging, pre-fabricated type requiring only assembly. Others will choose a model installed by professional contractors. Naturally, neither approach limits the size or professional qualities of the greenhouse.

Mr. Lance Walheim, who was the editor of the Ortho Book, *The World of Trees*, is an experienced greenhouse grower. Following are his comments regarding the purchase of a greenhouse of serious, almost professional quality:

"I would always have a cement floor contoured toward drainage holes leading to the outside. I think it's important to keep a greenhouse clean and to be able to hose it out as often as possible. Debris or soil can be hosed through large, closely spaced drainage holes. Cement floors also eliminate the problems of disease generated by damp open soil areas.

"Strong benches are essential. They should allow for maximum drainage or somehow prevent buildup of water which can harbor disease and promote wood rot.

"For glazing, I prefer corrugated fiberglass. It is durable, lightweight, and easy to handle.

Top, Mr. Floyd Pick wets gravel in early morning to raise humidity. Above, he checks growth of young pepper.

Prefab attached type greenhouse. Shade cloth rolls down like blinds.

"Propagation is easiest with a mist system and electric bottom heat. A separate compartment in the greenhouse is best for this purpose—it is much easier to control the environment on a smaller scale.

"Heating and cooling are the keys to successful greenhouse growing. Even heat distribution is best achieved by the perforated plastic sleeves or tubes underneath the benches. Actual placement of the heater becomes secondary because the heat can be directed by the tubes. Keep the heater low but not blowing directly on the plants.

"Cooling is a bit tougher. The three most common methods are wet walls (evaporative cooling), ventilation, and shading. A combination of the three usually works best. Evaporative coolers push cool air generated by the evaporating water. Another arrangement is to have the wet-wall and exhaust fans on opposite ends of the greenhouse—cool air is then pulled from one wall to the other."

Mr. Floyd Pick, another greenhouse enthusiast, chose a greenhouse kit. If you are considering this type, let his experience be a guide:

"I ordered the 12′×6′ model. It arrived in three packages. One package contained the fan, heater, and thermostat. The other two contained the redwood, fiberglass, and hardware. The total weight of the three boxes was about 270 lbs.

"The first stages of construction were probably the most difficult. I did 95% of the construction myself but I needed to get help a couple of times until the ridge brace connecting the frame sections was in place. My wife held a section in place until the connection could be made.

"Before the fiberglass panels were installed, I treated the frame with a stain and sealer. The frame is redwood which is decay and insect resistant to some degree. I believe this step will extend the life of the frame considerably. Where the wood braces are close to the earth, I painted with copper napthanate, greenish-colored wood preservative.

"The benches were bought separately. I ordered two that run the length of each side. Mine are stacked one on top of the other resembling bunk beds.

Detail of fan installation and electrical hookup made by Mr. Pick.

The opposite side of the greenhouse is for a raised bed. On the shelves will be my cactus and succulent collection, plus a few house plants. Seed propagation (heat cable, mist, and Gro-light fixture) will also take up some bench space. The raised bed is for vegetables —tomatoes, cucumbers, etc. I'm especially looking forward to growing vegetables next winter.

"Back 15 or 20 years I remember commenting that I'd like a greenhouse. It always seemed too expensive and time consuming. (So far, my total costs have been only $520.) The rising cost of supermarket produce is one reason I finally bought one. It may take a while but someday I expect to reduce my grocery bill.

"For me, the actual assembly was not difficult. It took about 50 hours in total. I believe anyone who is methodical and patient can do as well.

Greenhouse sources

Aluminum Greenhouses, Inc.
14615 Lorain Avenue
Cleveland, OH 44111
Freestanding and lean-to light weight models.

American Leisure Industries
Box 63
Deep River, CT 06417

Casa-planta
9489 Dayton Way
Beverly Hills, CA 90210
Inexpensive modular, vinyl covered.

Environmental Dynamics
P.O. Box 996
Sunnymead, CA 92388
Fiberglass prefabs with steel frame.

Gothic Arch Greenhouses
Box 1564
Mobile, AL 36601
Freestanding prefabs.

Ickes-Braun Glasshouses
P.O. Box 147
Deerfield, IL 60015
Complete supplies for building your own design.

Lord and Burnham
Irvington, NY 10533
All sizes and types.

Maco Home Greenhouses
Box 109
Scio, OR 97374
Inexpensive greenhouses.

McGregor Greenhouses
Box 36
Santa Cruz, CA 95063
Fiberglass prefabs.

National Greenhouse Company
P.O. Box 100
Pana, IL 62557
Freestanding models, many sizes.

J. A. Nearing Company
10788 Tucker Street
Beltsville, MD 20705
Aluminum greenhouses.

Pacific Coast Manufacturing Co.
430 Hurlingame Avenue
Redwood City, CA 94063
Greenhouse kits and supplies.

Redfern Greenhouses
55 Mount Hermon Road
Scotts Valley, CA 95060
Prefab lean-to and freestanding

Redwood Domes
P.O. Box 666
Santa Cruz, CA 95060
Geodesic dome greenhouses.

Peter Reimuller
Box 2666
Santa Cruz, CA 95060
Inexpensive vinyl-covered models.

Santa Barbara Greenhouses
390 Dawson Drive
Camarillo, CA 93010
Inexpensive fiberglass prefabs.

Sturdi-Built Manufacturing Co.
11304 S.W. Boones Ferry Road
Portland, OR 97219
Prefab home units.

Texas Greenhouse Company
2717 St. Louis Avenue
Fort Worth, TX 76110
Prefab aluminum and redwood units.

Turner Greenhouses
Box 1260
Goldsboro, NC 27530
Inexpensive greenhouses.

Vegetable Factory, Inc.
100 Court Street
Copiague, L.I., NY 11726
Aluminum frame, double pane acrylic glazing. Several models.

Verandel Company
Box 1568
Worcester, MA 01611
Inexpensive lean-to greenhouses.

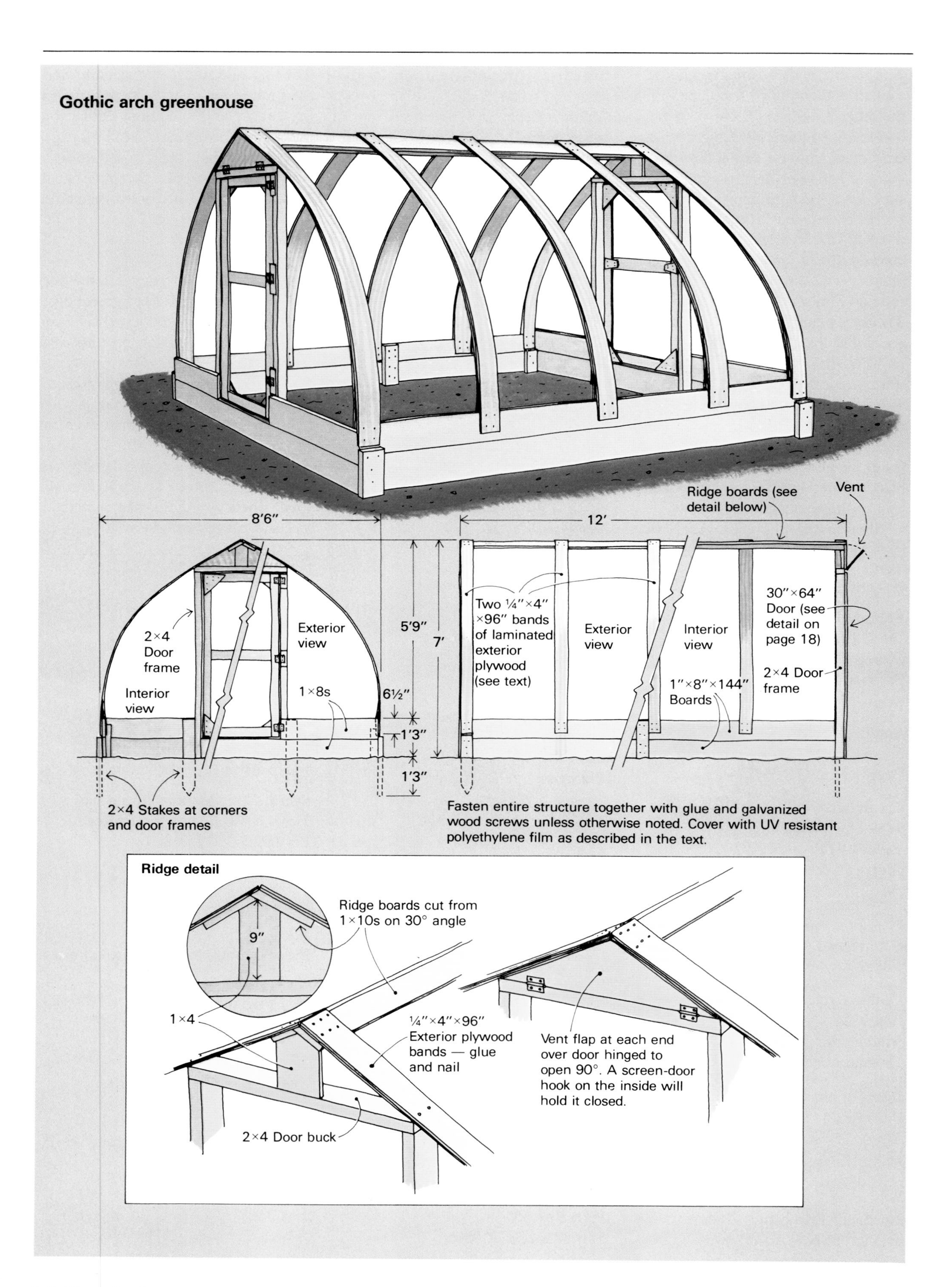
Gothic arch greenhouse
8'6"
12'
Ridge boards (see detail below)
Vent
5'9"
7'
6½"
1'3"
1'3"
2×4 Door frame
Interior view
Exterior view
1×8s
Two ¼"×4" ×96" bands of laminated exterior plywood (see text)
Exterior view
Interior view
1"×8"×144" Boards
30"×64" Door (see detail on page 18)
2×4 Door frame
2×4 Stakes at corners and door frames
Fasten entire structure together with glue and galvanized wood screws unless otherwise noted. Cover with UV resistant polyethylene film as described in the text.
Ridge detail
9"
Ridge boards cut from 1×10s on 30° angle
1×4
¼"×4"×96" Exterior plywood bands — glue and nail
Vent flap at each end over door hinged to open 90°. A screen-door hook on the inside will hold it closed.
2×4 Door buck

Gothic Arch

This model is well-suited to areas where there is just enough winter freezing to be troublesome to your plants or small potted fruit trees. It can be easily covered with polyethylene film or, for more permanence, with flat fiberglass panels. This greenhouse is also portable. (While this greenhouse is designed to be light weight and portable, it can be placed on a conventional foundation if you want more permanence.)

Begin by making a frame of two 1×8s cleated together that is 12 feet long and 8 feet 6 inches wide. Use wood treated with copper napthenate or other good preservative.

For the roof supports, cut 20 pieces of ¼-inch exterior grade plywood that are 4 inches wide and 8 feet long. Glue and nail each together in two sets—10 bands will form each of the sides—with galvanized nails, leaving the bottom 8 inches unglued and unnailed.

The next step is to frame in the end support walls and the doors. At each end, cut an opening 2 feet 9 inches wide in the center of the top board of the frame.

Notch two 6 foot lengths of 2×4s to fit flush with the bottom board of the frame. Nail on a 2 foot 9 inch door buck at the top and then nail each door frame into position.

For the ridge board, cut a 30° angle on each side of a 12 foot length of 2×4 and toenail it into place on the center of the door buck. To each side of the ridge board, nail a 12-foot 1×6. This is the support for the bands of plywood rafters.

Put the rafters in place with galvanized wood screws on the ridge line and nail and glue them around the frame. Start at one end with the band nailed and glued on the inside only. Curve it over the door frame and nail it there before screwing it into the ridge boards. Now nail and glue the outside flap to the frame. Complete both ends and then finish at the middle supports.

The gable openings above the doors at the ends are covered with pieces of ⅜-inch exterior grade plywood cut to fit. These should be hinged so they can open for added ventilation.

The doors for this light greenhouse are made from 2×2s with one cross brace at the center. Additional strength is given the door by nailing on triangular plywood braces, or gussets, at each corner. Hinge at the top, bottom and middle. Now, cover the doors with a polyethylene film that is resistant to ultraviolet damage and you have a greenhouse.

In windy areas, this greenhouse should be held (or anchored) to the ground. Set the greenhouse in the location you want and then drive two stakes 18 inches into the ground on each side of the door and two on each side of the framework. Fasten the stakes to the frame with wood screws.

A-Frame Greenhouse

The A-frame's chief advantage lies in its easy construction. This particular model is also relatively small and light weight which makes it portable if you have a few strong friends. It is also useful in areas that get a heavy snow load. This model is often covered on the outside with 8 mil plastic film of a type resistant to ultraviolet rays. For additional protection, which would be essential in any snow country, put another layer of ordinary 4 mil polyethylene inside to create a thermal barrier.

The base is made from four 10-foot pieces of 2×6 redwood or treated fir. (This greenhouse is also designed to be portable but it may also be placed on the conventional foundation described previously.) For the rafters and end walls, you need fifteen 10-foot lengths of 2×3. The ridge board and door are made from 1×4.

Put the frame together, using plywood gussets at the corners. To build, cut one rafter to fit and use it as the pattern for the nine other rafters. Build one wall with the 1×4 ridge board nailed to it, then stand and brace that wall in place. Then nail the other five rafters in place. With the whole structure still braced, nail in the diagonal braces, then finish the end walls. To provide proper venting, frame in a 10-inch diameter fan above the door and a louvered opening of the same size at the opposite end of the greenhouse.

A bench across the far end gives a good working space with ample headroom.

The structure should be securely anchored to the ground. One method is to use a screw-type fence anchor set into notches cut in the base and held with short pieces of rerod pushed through the screw eye.

This A-frame greenhouse features ease of construction and portability. The frame is 2×2-inch stock. Glazing is chicken-wire and polyethylene.

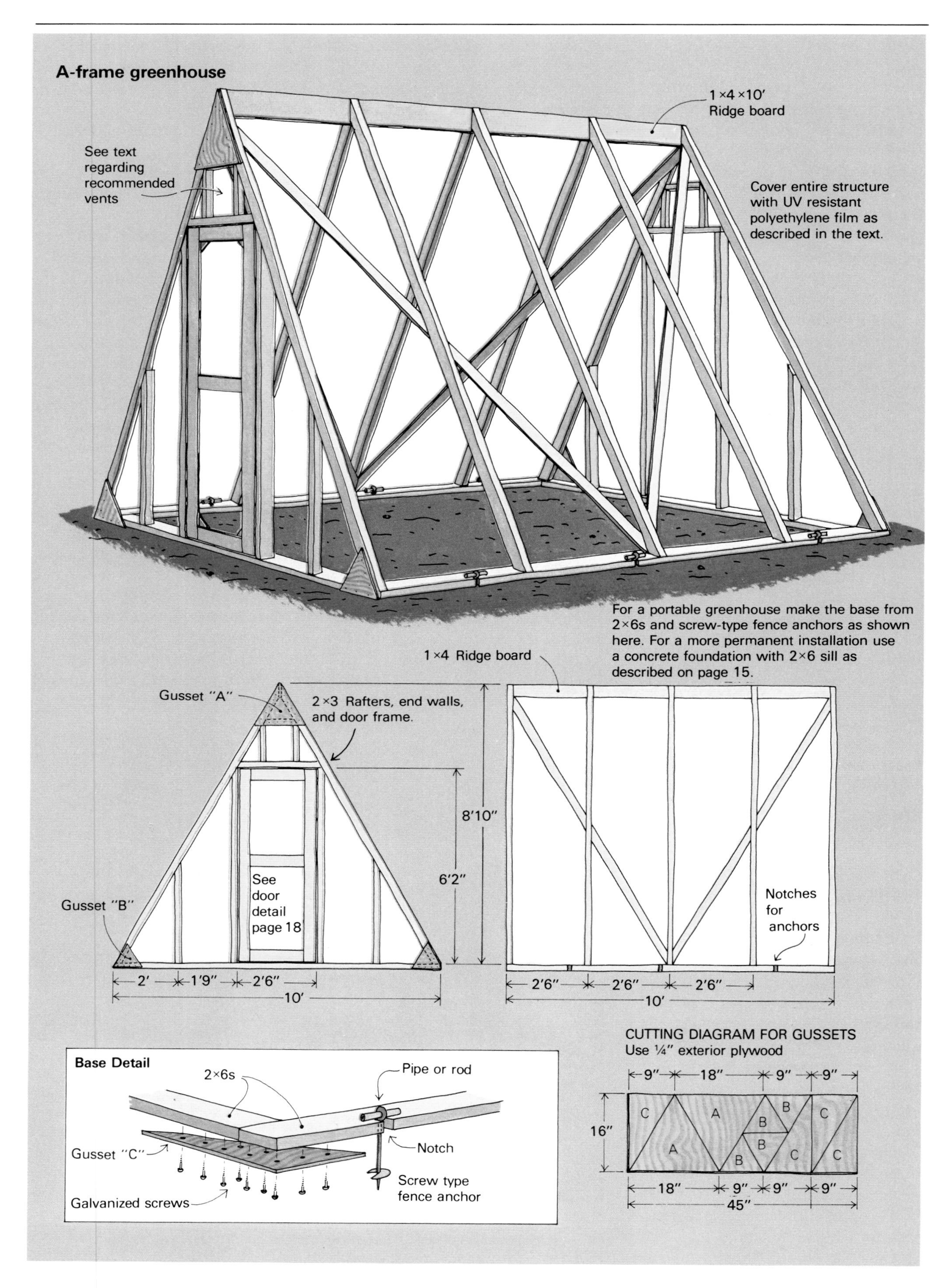
A-frame greenhouse
1×4×10′
Ridge board
See text regarding recommended vents
Cover entire structure with UV resistant polyethylene film as described in the text.
For a portable greenhouse make the base from 2×6s and screw-type fence anchors as shown here. For a more permanent installation use a concrete foundation with 2×6 sill as described on page 15.
1×4 Ridge board
Gusset "A"
2×3 Rafters, end walls, and door frame.
8′10″
6′2″
See door detail page 18
Gusset "B"
Notches for anchors
2′
1′9″
2′6″
10′
2′6″
2′6″
2′6″
10′
CUTTING DIAGRAM FOR GUSSETS
Use ¼″ exterior plywood
9″
18″
9″
9″
16″
18″
9″
9″
9″
45″
A
B
C
Base Detail
2×6s
Pipe or rod
Notch
Gusset "C"
Galvanized screws
Screw type fence anchor

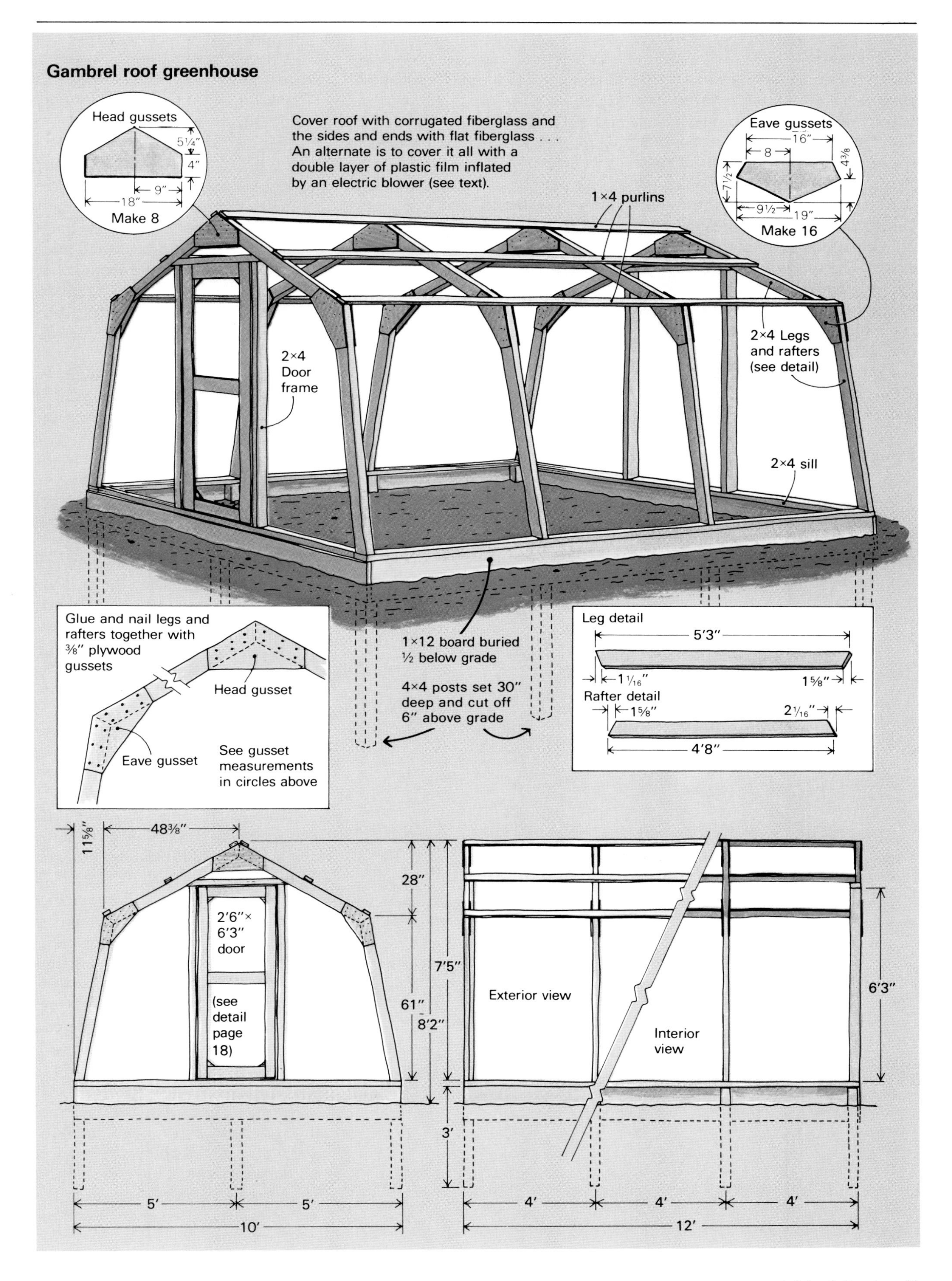
Gambrel roof greenhouse
Head gussets
5¼″
4″
9″
18″
Make 8
Cover roof with corrugated fiberglass and the sides and ends with flat fiberglass . . . An alternate is to cover it all with a double layer of plastic film inflated by an electric blower (see text).
1×4 purlins
Eave gussets
16″
8
4⅜
7½
9½
19″
Make 16
2×4 Door frame
2×4 Legs and rafters (see detail)
2×4 sill
Glue and nail legs and rafters together with ⅜″ plywood gussets
Head gusset
Eave gusset
See gusset measurements in circles above
1×12 board buried ½ below grade
4×4 posts set 30″ deep and cut off 6″ above grade
Leg detail
5′3″
1¹⁄₁₆″
1⅝″
Rafter detail
1⅝″
2¹⁄₁₆″
4′8″
11⅝″
48⅜″
2′6″× 6′3″ door
(see detail page 18)
28″
61″
7′5″
8′2″
3′
5′
5′
10′
Exterior view
Interior view
6′3″
4′
4′
4′
12′

Free-Standing Gambrel Roof Greenhouse

This type of greenhouse goes up in sections. It lends itself readily to either a polyethylene or fiberglass covering. This type of greenhouse, which is built similarly to barns, has considerable structural strength. It is excellent in country that has a heavy snowfall. One of the more time-consuming requirements is cutting the plywood gussets. To speed this up, cut one of each pattern as shown in the cutting diagram and then use it as a pattern to mark all the others. Also, carefully note the cutting diagram for the legs and rafters. After they are all cut, put the legs and rafters together using a waterproof glue with the gussets.

For a 10 by 12 foot greenhouse, the frame is constructed by sinking 4-foot long 4×4s about 3 feet into the ground. This leaves 12 inches exposed on which to nail the 1×12 redwood frame around the base. (This unit can also be placed on the previously described foundation for more permanence.) To make the frame level, drive the posts in about 30 inches and cut off the excess after you have put the frame in place and adjusted it until it is level. The posts go 6 feet apart down the sides and 5 feet apart across the front and back. Across the top of the 4×4 posts goes a 2×4 sill. Mark the sill where each leg and end support will go.

To frame up the greenhouse, put the preconstructed end walls in place first and brace securely. Put the two 1×4 purlins on the ridge, then put in the two center supports and hold them in place by nailing to the purlins. Double-check that everything is square before nailing. The structure is further strengthened with 1×4 purlins at the middle and lower edge of the roof.

If using two layers of plastic, the thermal layer of air between them can be maintained with the use of a small squirrel cage fan. Install it at one end near the ridge line by mounting it to a plywood panel suspended from the end rafter. Cut a hole in the plywood for the fan to draw in air and use flexible plastic tubing and a plastic pot with a hole cut in the bottom to direct the air between the two layers of plastic.

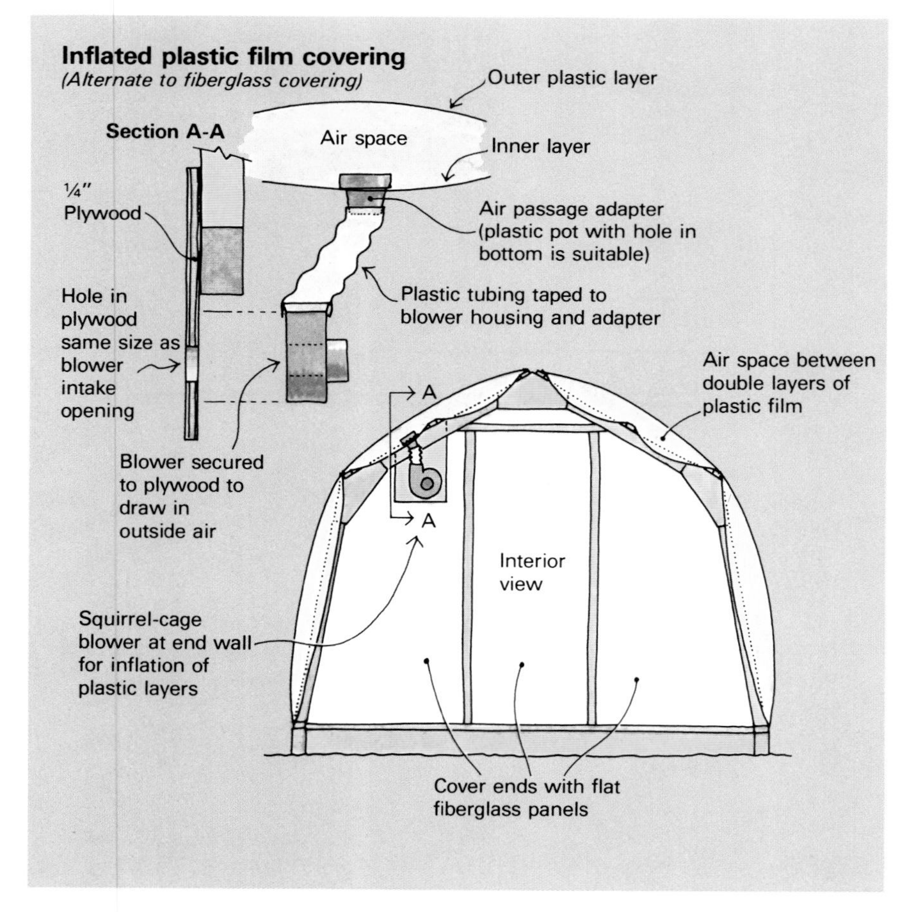

Simplified Gambrel Roof

Here is an excellent style of framing for a small greenhouse. The insider's trick to this one is finding and cutting the angles for the roof.

Start by laying out the foundation that is 8 by 12 feet. If you live in a dry enough climate, it can go directly on the ground with this lightweight building. It would be better, however, to put it on a concrete block foundation. Once the sill is in place, build the two side walls, making them 4 feet 10 inches high so that a 5-foot length of fiberglass siding will fully cover the bottom sill.

The angles for the roof rafters are best found by working on a piece of plywood 4 by 8 feet (the 8 feet is the width of the greenhouse). First, mark the center of the plywood near the lengthwise top of the sheet. Now you will diagram just one side of the roof and when those pieces are cut you will use them for the other side.

With a length of 2×4 about 4 feet long, trace its outline on the plywood at an angle of your choice for the first leg of the roof. Now trace another outline over to the center of the plywood sheet for the second leg of the roof. Where the two traced patterns intersect, draw a line connecting the two intersection points to give you the angle of cut. The angle where the top leg meets the ridge board is found by drawing a vertical line down through it.

Once all the rafter legs have been measured and cut, nail on a 1×4 at the top and bottom of them just as if you were constructing a wall on the ground. When you're done, you'll have four roof sections. Put both lower sections on top of the wall and brace them temporarily in place. To tie them together and support them, run a cross brace between each one at the top. Now put the two top components in place and nail. The end walls are made with 2×4s under each roof angle and under the center.

A door can be cut to fit from 1×4s and covered with fiberglass. The structure can be anchored, if not on a foundation, by drilling holes every 4 feet through the bottom plate and sill and driving a 3-foot length of rerod into the ground through the holes. Bend the top 2 inches at a 90° angle.

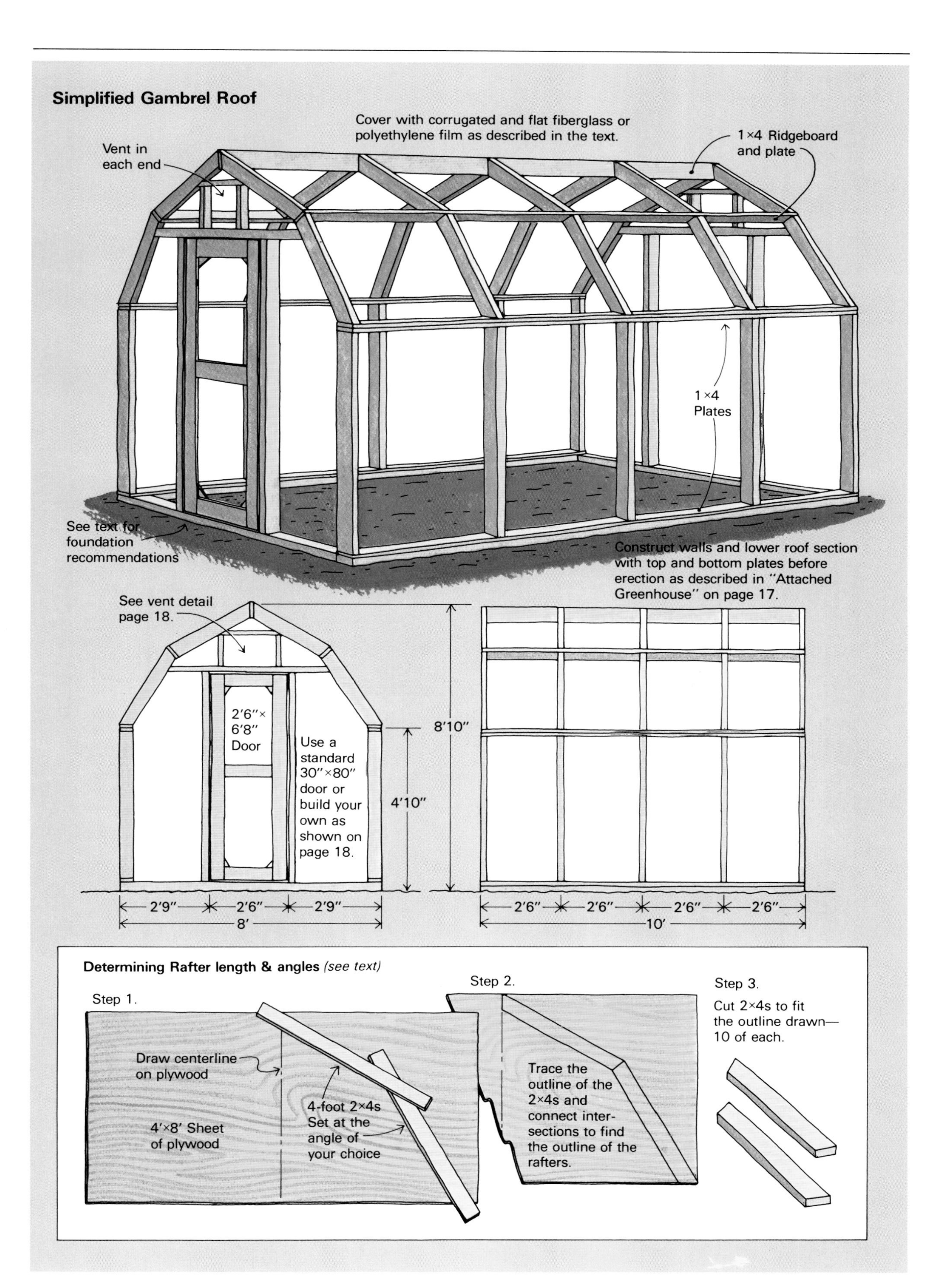

Simplified Gambrel Roof
Cover with corrugated and flat fiberglass or polyethylene film as described in the text.
Vent in each end
1×4 Ridgeboard and plate
1×4 Plates
See text for foundation recommendations
Construct walls and lower roof section with top and bottom plates before erection as described in "Attached Greenhouse" on page 17.
See vent detail page 18.
2'6"× 6'8" Door
Use a standard 30"×80" door or build your own as shown on page 18.
8'10"
4'10"
2'9"
2'6"
2'9"
8'
2'6"
2'6"
2'6"
2'6"
10'
Determining Rafter length & angles (see text)
Step 1.
Draw centerline on plywood
4'×8' Sheet of plywood
4-foot 2×4s Set at the angle of your choice
Step 2.
Trace the outline of the 2×4s and connect intersections to find the outline of the rafters.
Step 3.
Cut 2×4s to fit the outline drawn—10 of each.

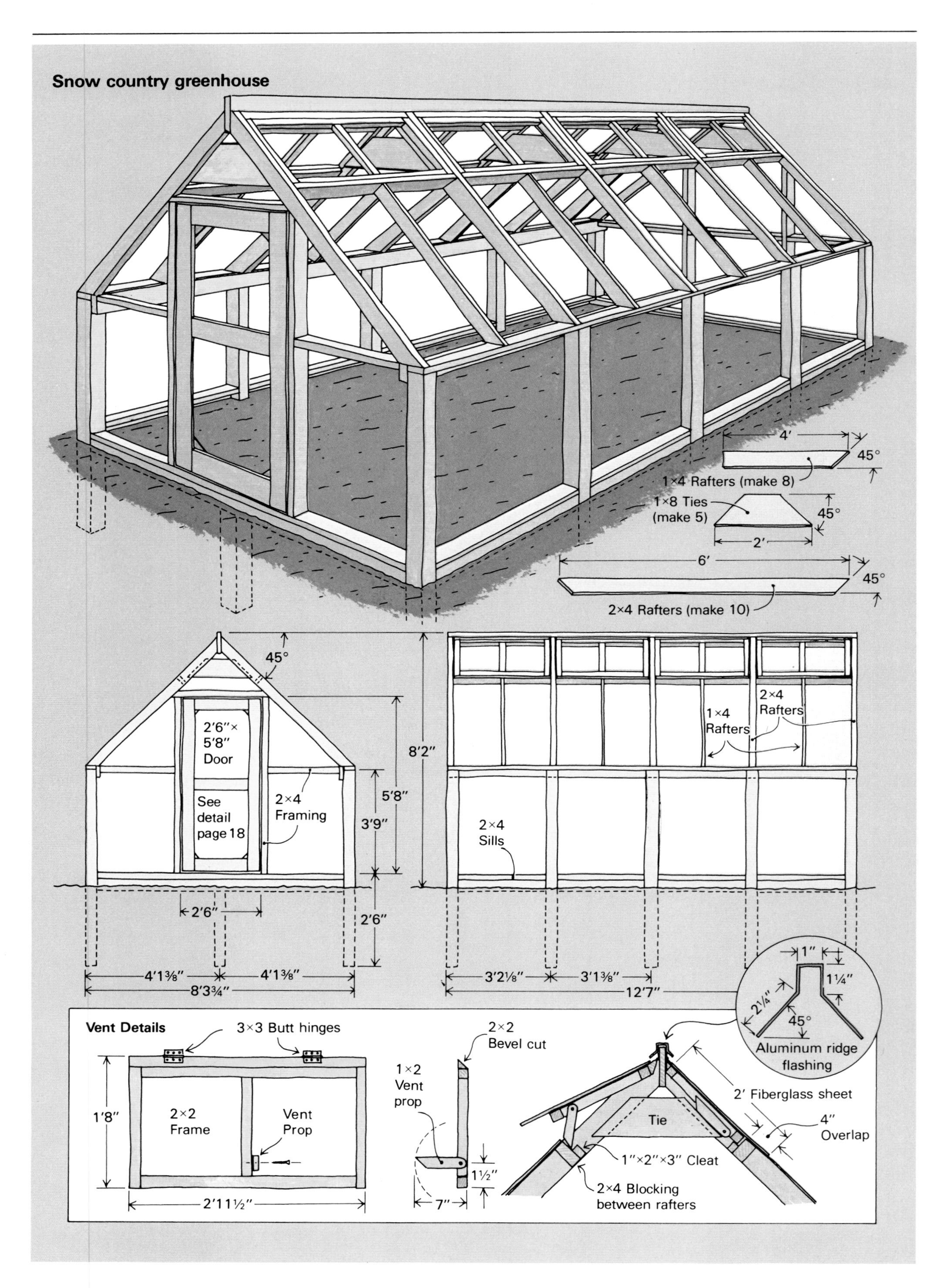

Snow country greenhouse
4'
45°
1×4 Rafters (make 8)
1×8 Ties (make 5)
45°
2'
6'
45°
2×4 Rafters (make 10)
45°
2'6"× 5'8" Door
See detail page 18
2×4 Framing
5'8"
3'9"
8'2"
2'6"
2'6"
4'1⅜"
4'1⅜"
8'3¾"
1×4 Rafters
2×4 Rafters
2×4 Sills
3'2⅛"
3'1⅜"
12'7"
1"
1¼"
2¼"
45°
Aluminum ridge flashing
Vent Details
3×3 Butt hinges
1'8"
2×2 Frame
Vent Prop
2'11½"
1×2 Vent prop
2×2 Bevel cut
1½"
7"
2' Fiberglass sheet
Tie
4" Overlap
1"×2"×3" Cleat
2×4 Blocking between rafters

Snow Country Greenhouse

This greenhouse has a steep A-frame roof that will shed snow quickly. It also has a continuous line of roof vents for natural cooling in the summer. The University of Connecticut plan calls for ten pressure-treated posts to be sunk about 2½ feet in the ground with 3 feet 9 inches left above ground. To get these exact measurements, first sink the posts and then use a line level before cutting the tops off to the required height. It is important also that the posts be set the required distance apart of 8 feet 3¾ inches if the rafters are to fit smoothly. Each 2×4 rafter is 6 feet long with a 45° angle at both ends. The 1×4 rafters are 4 feet long with a 45° angle at the bottom.

After the posts are in place, put the 2×4 continuous top plate all around on top of the posts. Next put on the 2×4 side plate which helps support the rafter ends.

Then frame in the doors at both ends and use that frame to support the end rafters. After nailing the end rafters to the 1×8 ridge board, put up the other rafters, spaced 3 feet 1⅜ inches on center.

The 2×4 blocking is added to frame the vent openings and then the 1×4 rafters are toe-nailed into place, centered on the blocking.

The vents are framed with 2×2 and cut according to the diagram to fit between each rafter.

Benches and Potting Areas

Ideally, the benches and cabinets inside a greenhouse can be both functional and beautiful. They should be designed for your own needs, taking into consideration your height, your reach and your girth. For example, a heavy-set person who has difficulty in bending should not be trying to reach across a wide bench or under it to care for plants there.

The benches should also provide a good display area for the plants and be open to the maximum amount of light. They should be constructed in a manner that allows air to circulate freely through them and among the plants. You should keep a space between the back of the bench and the greenhouse wall for good air flow.

Generally, benches are 32 to 36 inches wide if they can be reached from only one side, and 42 to 48 inches wide if they run down the center of the greenhouse. For the sake of efficiency, the aisles should take up only between one-fourth and one-third of the total floor area. Again, adjust this rule of thumb to your special needs.

Different Bench Styles

The most common arrangement is simply a continuous bench that runs around the sides of the greenhouse. A small sink and potting area are often built into the bench.

One variation on the straight and level bench is the stairstep. This gives the grower more display room. Steps should face south to catch the most sunlight and that sometimes means too much direct light. Plants will have to be turned regularly unless you put them against a white wall to get reflected light. Shade-loving plants can go under the stair-step bench.

A different bench arrangement is the "peninsula," where a series of benches protrude towards the center like fingers or peninsulas. Although time-consuming to build, these are better for larger greenhouses because they provide a great amount of bench area. In this style, the center aisle may be 3 to 4 feet wide and the small aisles 18 to 24 inches wide. The bench tops are 42 to 48 inches wide. A reminder here: When installing benches, make sure they are on firm supports, such as bricks or concrete pads, and never just on the ground.

Some Basic Benches

An attractive and practical greenhouse bench is made from 2×4s with a top of 1×4s. The top can be as much as 36 inches wide but the support structure is no more than 30 inches wide to keep the legs out of your way. Lay the 2×4 legs on a flat surface such as a driveway or garage floor. Put them 4 feet apart on center and nail a 2×4 rail flush with the top. Use a square to make sure the legs are perpendicular to the rail. If your bench is 16 feet or less long, you should be able to buy one board for the rail. Otherwise, use notched joints to connect two or more boards.

Make a duplicate of this side and you have the front and back supports for the bench. Put them in place in your greenhouse and tie them together with a 2×4 brace inside the top of each leg and another halfway down. Remember, this substructure should not be more than 30 inches wide.

If you cannot tie this bench to either end of your greenhouse, it is advisable to use more braces underneath. Use 2×4s running from the center of a lower brace to a top brace. Cut bird's mouth openings in each for a tight, flush fit to the cross braces.

Once the frame is in place, cover the top with redwood 1×4s spaced an

inch apart. Allow a 6-inch overhang in front to keep your feet away from the legs. Give the top a finished look by nailing a strip of 1×1 half-round molding along the protruding ends. If you want to provide a lip to prevent pots from accidentally being brushed off, use a 1×2 for the facing.

For an attractive variation on this bench, one with a smoother appearance, use lap joints to tie the legs and the top rail together. If you don't have a table saw with a dado blade, make laps by marking each piece, cutting halfway through with a saw and then chiseling out the lap area. The top cross braces can be nailed directly to the inside of each leg where they are hidden, but the lower cross braces should be lap jointed for a truly finished effect.

The Component Bench

This type of bench can be built in components and readily adapts itself to any length. Build the support structure with 2×4s for the front and back legs and clasp each leg at the top between two 2×4s extending 6 inches beyond the front leg. One-third the distance up from the bottom of each leg, cut lap joints on the inside to accept 2×2 rails. These will strengthen the bench and also provide lower shelf supports. When the units are all cut and together, place them in the greenhouse and use finishing nails to put on the top of 1×4s spaced an inch apart.

If the bench is too long for single lengths of the 1×4 top, then put the joints on alternate legs so you do not have to trust all on one support.

Other Bench Styles

There are numerous other types of benches, including some that use ⅜-inch cement asbestos board, either corrugated or flat, to provide a solid top. These are primarily used for planting directly into soil on top of the bench. There are problems with this practice, however, including waterlogging of the plants and diseases spawning in the wet soil. Some gardeners use such benches to hold soaked vermiculite that keeps potted plants resting on top wet for several days.

If you want to use benches filled with soil, use corrugated asbestos because of its strength. Sometimes wire is laid across these corrugated boards to keep the pots from tipping and the boards are sloped slightly to carry away water.

Pipe-framed benches commonly have 1¼-inch galvanized pipe embedded in concrete piers. These pier forms could be made from half-gallon milk cartons. Set the complete framework in the forms and brace it while you check the level before pouring concrete.

Benches can also be quickly installed using cinder blocks on end and a framework of pipe or 2×4s. The top can be asbestos board or, for a really simple bench, just unroll a length of snow fence onto the rails.

Widely used in many greenhouses is the wiremesh top. It provides excellent circulation but sagging problems persist. To help minimize them, put cross supports every 2 feet. Cover the exposed ends of the wire where stapled with a 1×4.

The Greenhouse Potting Area

A greenhouse and a potting area should go hand-in-hand. Some people prefer the potting area outside but near the greenhouse, such as in some type of a lath structure. Others, especially those who are snowed upon for much of the winter, want it protected and warm, in the greenhouse itself. If you decide to have the potting area in the greenhouse, put it in the northeast corner where it will block the least amount of sun.

The potting area should meet several basic needs: a flat and solid place with sides 4 to 6 inches high to keep soil from spilling over; a handy place above the bench for tools; and room under the bench to keep soil mixes, fertilizers and pest sprays. A small sink is convenient here but not a necessity. If you do put in a sink, search for a used one in junk stores. It will do fine for about a third the price of a new one.

The sink can be set directly into the bench by resting it on two 2×4 braces. The sink top should be flush with the bench top for easy cleanup. Most codes require that the sink drain be tied into your house system, but since so little water is normally run through there, you may be able to pipe it directly onto a nearby plant or tree. In snow country the drain will have to stay below the freezing level and you may want to run it into a dry well filled with stones or tap it into the sprinkler pipes under the lawn. Check your local code requirements before you put in that sink.

With a bench already installed in a greenhouse, shelves can be made underneath by running 1×4 slats across the lower braces. Keep them spaced for good air circulation.

It's a good idea to keep the lower shelves protected with cabinet doors, particularly if small children are apt to wander in and start making mud pies with the fertilizers and soils kept underneath. Good cabinet doors are made just like a gate and from the same material as the bench top. Lay out two 1×4s about 18 inches apart and put on vertical 1×4 strips, leaving a 1-inch space between each. Don't nail until everything is laid out so you can make any adjustments for even spacing.

The vertical slats should fit under the bench top and against the top rail. Use a carpenter's square as you nail the slats in place with finishing nails. After they are on, turn the door over and check the square again. Cut a diagonal bracing and put it in place, with one end against the lower hinge. After it is hung on hinges, use magnetic catches or a bolt to fasten it in front.

Overhead cabinets can be made from 1×12 redwood cut to fit between the bench and the eave of your greenhouse. A handy cabinet is 3 feet wide and made like a box with simple butt joints that are nailed and glued. Put several shelves 6, 12 and 18 inches apart to handle your different storage needs. When the shelves are in, back the boxes with a piece of Masonite or other rigid material. If you want the back open for more light, use galvanized angle braces inside all corners.

If you have an outside wall to mount these boxes on, you do not need a backing or braces. Cut a 2×4 to fit across the inside of the box at the top. Fasten that 2×4 to the wall with lag screws sunk into the studs, and then hang the box from it. it. Put another 2×4 support under the lowest shelf to keep the box from swaying. Hold it in place with one screw through the top of the box into the wall support. Do the same at the bottom. The boxes can be hung horizontally rather than vertically if you prefer.

If you want cabinet doors, cut them to fit from ½-inch plywood and install with butt hinges.

Portable Work Bench

If you don't have a great deal of room in your greenhouse but still need to work in there, try a combination of two collapsible tables and a portable potting bench.

The greenhouse can also provide a much needed respite for ailing house plants, especially those that suffer from low light levels and dryness.

The folding tables are cut from ¾-inch exterior grade plywood that has been treated with a water seal and painted. Each table is no wider than the height of the potting bench. The table, when folded down, should clear the floor by at least an inch. You also need to get past the table when it is folded out.

The plywood top is hinged to the top rail of the bench. Under the front of the table, screw in a 2×4 and then attach two legs made of 2×2, with hinges. Put a cross support between the legs halfway down, using screws and glue. When you are not using the table, the legs fold up and the top drops down. If necessary, use magnetic catches to hold the legs up when the table is folded.

Put two of these tables beside each other with a 20-inch space in between. The portable potting board may be 24 inches wide, allowing a 2-inch overlap on each side. All dimensions can be reduced if your space is tight.

Make the base of the potting board from two 1×12 pieces of redwood. Tie the base together with 2×2 cleats underneath that are set in 2 inches from each side to keep the potting board from slipping when set between the two foldout tables. Make the sides from 1x6 redwood. You can use a coffee can or similar round object to mark the round ends for cutting.

Tool Rack

Above the potting area and between the two hanging cabinets is a good place for putting tools. Here they are easy to reach and replace so they won't clutter up your work area.

One type of tool rack is made by cutting a piece of peg board to fit the area and framing all the edges on the back with 1×2 furring strips, including one down the center. This is to keep the peg board away from the wall so you can insert the metal tool hangers. Put vertical 2×2s on each side and then glue and nail a 1×2 across the bottom to make a narrow shelf. Come up 6 inches from that and put a 1×2 across the front as the retainer for the tools. These racks are ideal for holding the variety of small trowels, shears, scissors, spoons and brushes that go with potting. You can add one more shelf above if necessary and then hang the heavier and less frequently used tools and supplies there.

Greenhouse Shelves

Once all the benches in the greenhouse are filled, you start looking for more room. Plants are commonly hung in individual pots, but a few suspended shelves will give you much more room.

One simple but effective way to hang several pots of the same size at once is to build a rack from 2×2s. Each rack should be as long as the overhead supports are spaced, usually 2 or 4 feet on center.

To make the racks, lay out two lengths of 2×2 and then nail on 2×2 cross pieces spaced just enough apart to catch the pots near the top. Suspend the framework with thin wires from eyebolts. If the shelves are 4 feet or longer, run support wires down to their center.

For a more finished appearance, each crosspiece can be lap jointed and painted.

A variation on this shelf is a rack 8 to 12 inches wide and made from 2×2s and lath strips. For a shelf 8 inches wide, cut the 2×2 supports 12 inches long and space every 12 inches. Nail on the lath strips with ½ inch of space between each. To keep the pots from tipping over, put vertical pieces of 2×2 on the end of each undersupport, using a lap joint for added rigidity. Across the top add a lath rail.

A Final Chore

When your crystal palace is constructed, there is still one more important job to do before you start on your first greenhouse growing project. You should completely sterilize the interior of the greenhouse.

Probably the quickest, easiest, cheapest and safest way is to wash everything down with a broom and a bucket of water that has a pint of liquid household bleach such as Chlorox added. Be sure to get into all the crevices and crannies of benches, side walls and floors.

Big EARL

Growing Techniques

Techniques for controlling greenhouse temperatures, heating, cooling, shading. How to control humidity, build mist systems, mix soils.

Growing plants in a greenhouse is different in several respects from growing plants outside. It is subject to wide extremes in temperature on the outside but must maintain a good climate inside if the plants are to grow well. In the summer, sunlight can build the temperature to suffocating levels unless the greenhouse is properly ventilated and cooled. In the winter, it's a problem to know just how much heat you need. Unless you have sealed the house tightly and insulated the outside or used a double wall inside, heat will flow out of the greenhouse at an alarming—and costly—rate. These problems can be compounded by the necessity of maintaining a proper level of humidity.

Along with temperature and humidity, several other factors have to be considered: the kind and amount of ventilation, the amount of light—both natural and artificial—the plants will have, and the soil and air moisture. These variations and combinations are going to determine how successful you are in producing those beautiful big tomatoes, or poinsettias for Christmas. The greenhouse is a place where you'll want to grow plants that originated in different parts of the world and grow naturally under different conditions.

The best rule to follow is to learn as much as you can about the origin and preferences of the plants you want to grow, especially what the best natural conditions are for each variety, and then duplicate those conditions as nearly as you can in the greenhouse. If you want to grow a plant from a tropical rain forest and another from the desert, make as good a compromise with these natural conditions as you can.

All of these problems, however, can be overcome by the careful and determined greenhouse gardener.

Temperature in the Greenhouse

No matter if you live North, East, South or West, heating the air or cooling it will require careful planning and understanding. Most of us in this country think of our greenhouse primarily as a place to grow plants in the wintertime, so we will talk about heating first.

The two basic considerations in

Two thermostats for one greenhouse are helpful. One controls a heater and the other a cooling fan. Seedlings, opposite page and above, are tomatoes.

heating a greenhouse are to provide enough heat and to distribute it evenly, all at a reasonable cost.

The entire system should be automatic so you don't have to be around nursing it all the time. And the heating system should be as simple and straightforward as possible to minimize problems. It should also be designed to use the cheapest available fuel.

In considering the above, use as many solar heating techniques as you can. Sunlight is still free (and untaxed) so make use of it. Several means of capturing and storing solar heat are discussed in the solar greenhouse section.

Before you install any type of heat system, double-check for cracks around vents, doors and glazing panes. These small leaks allow great amounts of heat to escape and it's just like letting dollar bills fly out the window. Line them with 4 mil polyethylene film. The inner layer should be 1 to 6 inches away from the glazing for good results. An air space of less than ¾ inch is not only inefficient but may positively speed the heat loss through convection, as a chimney can.

Above, shielded thermometer, thermostat, and humidistat are the basic guides to greenhouse climate control. Above left, a typical gas-fired automatic greenhouse heater. Left, workers at Planting Fields Arboretum, Oyster Bay, New York, install an internal insulating layer of polyethylene. The dead air space between the glass and plastic is an excellent insulator that will significantly reduce winter heating costs.

Estimating Heating Needs

Use this method to determine the size of heater your greenhouse needs:

First, figure the total surface area (SA). You get this by multiplying length times height of each wall and the roof. For instance, one 6×8 foot wall has 48 square feet. Don't count the floor. Add all the other surfaces together and the result is the total area in square feet.

Second, calculate the degree rise (DR), which is the difference between the coldest outdoor temperature recorded in the past several years and the temperature you want to maintain in the greenhouse. Get the low temperature from the weather bureau. If you want to maintain a greenhouse temperature of 55° F (13° C) and the lowest expected temperature is 15° F (-9° C), you have a rise of 40° F (4° C).

Now consider the insulating factors (IF) for the type of glazing in your greenhouse:

Glazing	*Calm*	*Windy*
Glass	1.5	1.8
Fiberglass or polyethylene	1.2	1.4
Double layer (glass/plastic)	8.0	1.0

Now start multiplying: SA×DR×IF= heat loss per hour in British thermal units (Btu). The heater output for your greenhouse should be equal to the heat loss you just calculated.

Most heaters are labeled with their rated Btu output but you can convert your Btu findings to kilowatts for electric heaters by dividing by 3,413.

In making the final decision on your heater, remember that very low outside temperatures don't come along every year: you can probably get by with a smaller heater and save more money. You can also install a battery-operated alarm in case the temperature does fall suddenly or your heating system fails.

Whatever type of heater you have—coal, wood, gas, electric—you must keep the air in the greenhouse moving to prevent all the heat from collecting at the top of the roof. That is why the heater with a combination fan and thermostat is so widely used. Other-

wise, use the cheapest heating fuel available to you and install a small fan near the top of the roof to circulate the air downward.

The thermostat that will run both the heater and the summer vent fans should be located where it will not be in direct sunlight. It is commonly mounted on the wall under a shelf or in a small box to protect it.

A relatively new concept in heating is the use of infrared waves. One commercial greenhouse we know of has been using gas-fired overhead infrared heaters since 1976 with an estimated fuel savings of 60 to 65 percent compared with normal gas-fired heaters. Infrared heating is totally different from conventional heating. Conventional heaters warm the air which in turn warms the plants. Infrared radiation, a form of electromagnetic energy, travels in a straight line until it hits a solid object which absorbs that energy. In a greenhouse the energy hits plants and warms them, not the surrounding air. The units look something like fluorescent fixtures and can hang close to plants without harming them. Reflectors direct the heat in uniform patterns to ensure all corners of the greenhouse are covered.

Top, a thermocouple type automatic vent. Left, a small fan for air circulation. Above, electric vent control coupled to thermostat.

Cooling the Greenhouse

In much of the country, cooling the greenhouse in the summer is a greater problem than heating it in winter. In the northern latitudes, you may not have a cooling problem: open vents in the wall and roof may be enough. This is probably true if the summer temperatures around your area rarely exceed 80° F (27° C). But if you have long periods with higher temperatures, plan on installing some cooling devices.

There are two basic rules for keeping a greenhouse cool: first, you minimize the heat buildup by shading and second, you use fans to draw the cooler outside air in while blowing out the hot greenhouse air.

Like heating, the entire fan system should be automatic. Fans should all be hooked to thermostats so they will kick on when the temperature rises beyond a certain point. It's better to buy a two-speed fan so you can set the air exchange to half during the less

Top left—Thermometers placed among the plants show actual temperatures of the air around the plants. Top right—a maximum/minimum thermometer. The mercury pushes pins that stop at peak temperatures. Above—the interior effect of an aluminum shading screen. Right—with trellis in place, natural shading will be provided by plants which will be trained to grow up the trellis.

extreme months of spring and fall. The thermostats should also be made especially for greenhouses so they will not be damaged by high humidity. Some thermostat settings are not too accurate: check them by placing two or three thermometers around your greenhouse.

In addition to the fans, use thermal pistons to open and close vents automatically. These pistons expand with heat to open vents and then contract when the temperature drops. They come with dials so you can set them to your needs.

Shading

Greenhouses are sometimes shaded during the hot months. Opaque plastic, bamboo or aluminum screens can be mounted on the roof and rolled down when protection is needed. These are also useful to protect glass roofs in areas with heavy hailstorms. Green vinyl comes in rolls and can be cut to fit inside your windows. Wet the windows and then apply the plastic with a squeegee.

More exact shade protection can be provided by buying Saran or other shade cloth from greenhouse supply stores. These cloths are rated by the density or thread count to provide shade, and range from 30 to 92 percent. They are equipped with grommets to tie them securely over greenhouse roofs.

Other gardeners whitewash their greenhouse roofs in the summer and count on the winter rains to wash it away. The results are not particularly attractive. Other solutions are to build lightweight lath covers to lay up on the roofs, or lay on panels of green fiberglass framed with 2×2s. A more natural shade can come from planting sunflowers or pole beans on the south side of the greenhouse and training them over the roof.

Cooling Devices

Shading helps, but face it: In most parts of this country you need some artificial cooling for a really effective greenhouse. One of the best at a low price is the evaporative cooler, commonly called a swamp cooler. You can buy one, or make your own for a

A thermostatically controlled cooler.

fraction of the price. The basic principle is simple: A fan draws outside air through a constantly wetted pad which further cools the air and increases the humidity at the same time.

In setting this up, you're going to have to recall some basic math. A small calculator makes it fast and painless. First, fans are rated in cubic feet per minute (cfm), which means how many cubic feet of air they can move every minute. To find the cubic feet of space in your greenhouse so you can buy the right size fan, multiply the length and the width of the greenhouse by the *average* height of the roof. This height often comes close to 10 feet, which makes the calculation a little easier. An 8×12-foot greenhouse would have 96 square feet of floor. Multiply this by your average roof height, say 10 feet, which gives you a volume of 960 cubic feet.

Commercial greenhouses plan on exchanging all the air inside every minute. But the home greenhouse, with a smaller volume that heats up much faster, should exchange the air twice a minute. So, if your greenhouse has a volume of 960 cubic feet, you want a fan that will move twice that amount of air every minute, or about 2,000 cfm.

This fan should be mounted close to the top of the roof, usually over the door, to pull out the hottest air. The cooling pad should be located at the opposite end of the greenhouse and ideally at the same level as the plants. The cooling is done by pulling air through a constantly wet pad of aspen shavings, excelsior or plastic.

The size of the pad for your greenhouse is important. It is determined by dividing the needed air flow by 150. Thus, the 8×12 foot greenhouse needing air exchange of 2,000 cfm would require about 13 square feet of pad (2,000 ÷ 150 = 13.3). An effective pad must be continuous across the entire wall.

Aspen pads can be bought anywhere replacement pads for swamp coolers are sold. The pad should be cut to size and then clamped between wire mesh to prevent it from sagging. Cut the greenhouse wall opening to size and frame it with 2×4 redwood or some other wood treated with a preservative. On the lower support, mount a section of rain gutter angled slightly for water runoff. Fasten the screen and pad in place between the frame with screws and washers for easy removal.

At the lower end of the rain gutter, stand a plastic garbage can with a circulating pump that will supply about ⅓ of a gallon per minute per lineal foot

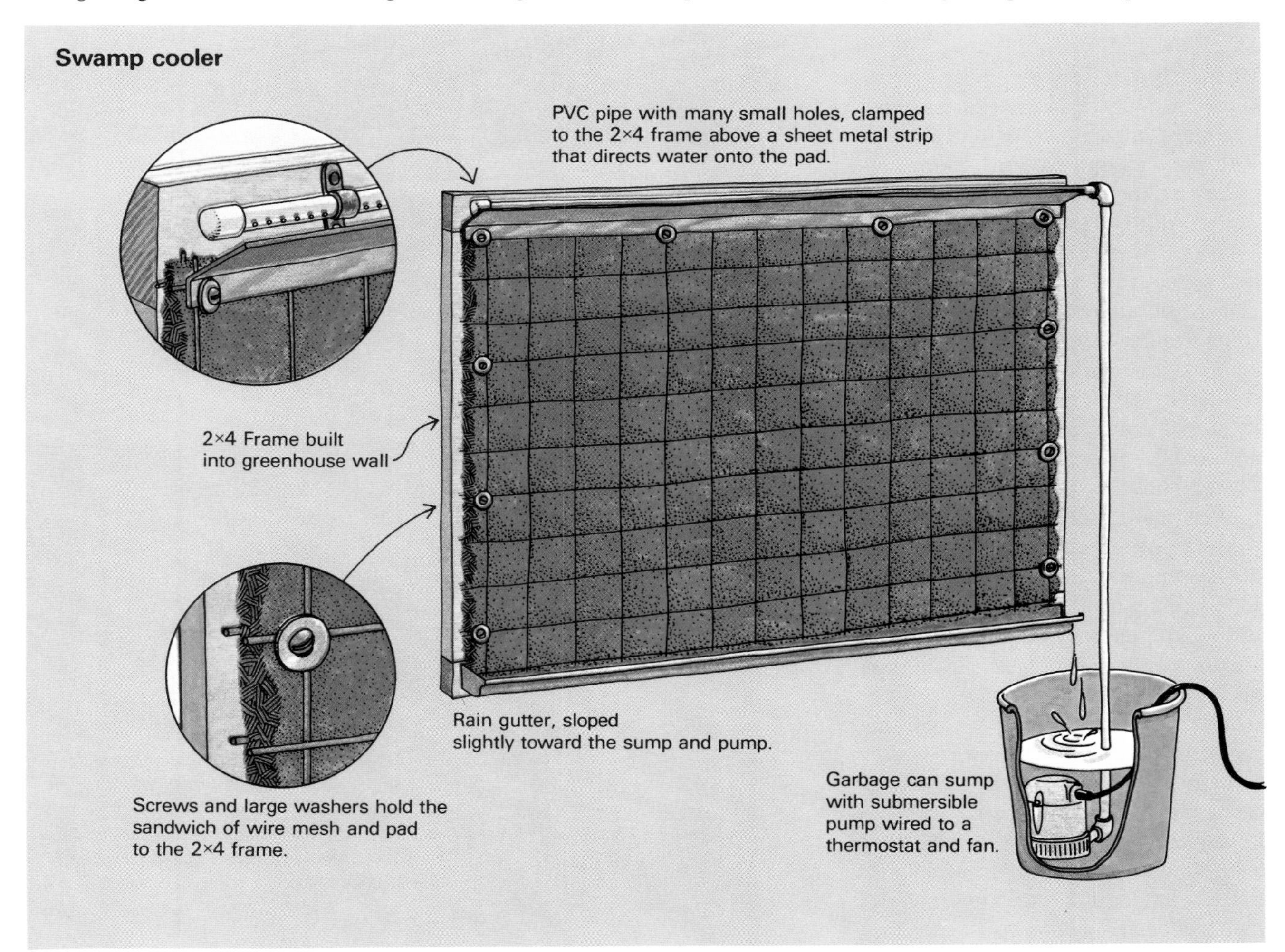

of pad, regardless of the pad's height. The sump, or garbage can, should have a capacity of 1¼ gallons for each lineal foot of pad in order to hold the water that drains back when the system stops.

The water is distributed by a PVC pipe clamped to the 2×4 just above the pad. Drill a close series of ⅛-inch holes and for better distribution of the water, put a small strip of sheet metal under the pipe to spread the water onto the pad.

The pump and fan are generally hooked to the same thermostat so they will start at the same time. A slightly more sophisticated hookup is in two stages: The fan starts when the temperature hits 70° F (21° C) and the water starts moving when the temperature reaches 80° F (27° C). A reminder: The fan will draw air through any crack in the greenhouse so make sure it is tightly sealed to insure that all the air comes through the pad only.

Don't forget to replace this section of the greenhouse wall for the winter, and remember to seal it in well.

Humidity Control

If the humidity in the greenhouse is too low, the plants will suffer and show it with poor growth patterns. High humidity makes many plants grow better but when it is over 90 percent for any length of time, there is a high risk of leaf mold and stem rot.

Low humidity is generally corrected by misting or watering the floor two or three times a day to build up water content in the air. Only in severely dry areas would a humidifier be needed in a greenhouse, particularly if a pad or swamp cooler is used.

Too much humidity is the usual problem, when roof and walls are so loaded with condensation that it seems to be raining inside. If the level is high during the day but the leaves have a chance to dry out at nightfall, the risk to the plants is not too severe. It is when the leaves are damp through the night that real problems can arise.

Condensation problems often occur during cold weather. The air in the greenhouse flows along the cold windows and cools so rapidly it can no longer hold its moisture. It then condenses out onto the plastic.

Top, a mist spray keeps humidity high. Usually automatic, the solenoid valve (above middle) connects timer and water flow. Left, a dry bulb/wet bulb humidistat. Above, humidifiers add water to air without dripping.

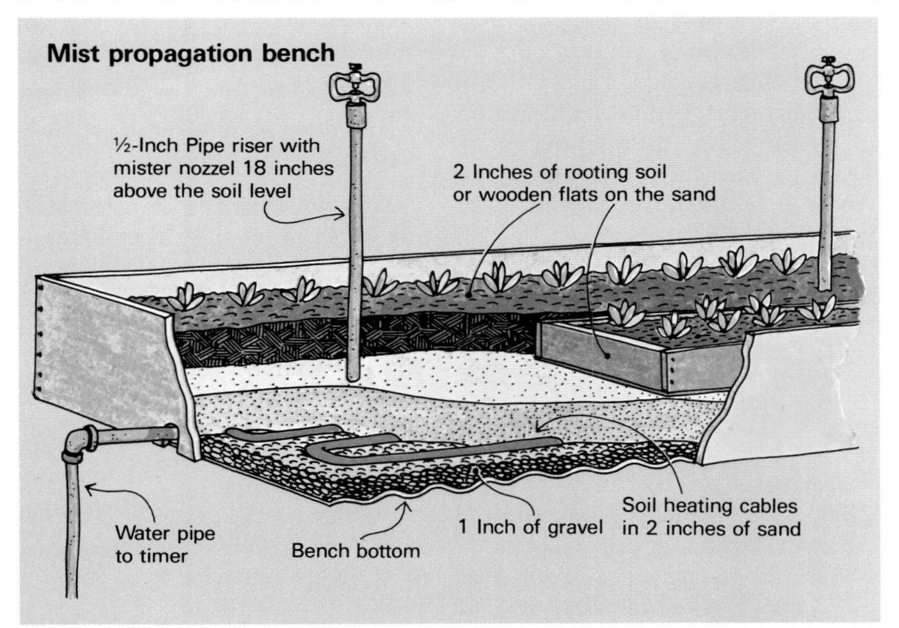

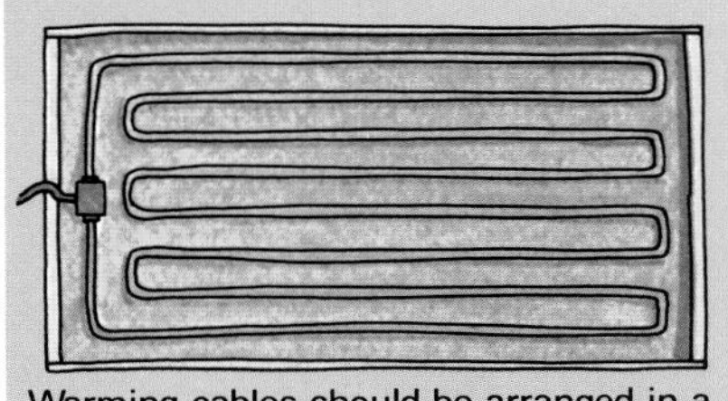

Warming cables should be arranged in a manner as shown here. Spaces should be of equal widths and the cable must never cross itself.

Time clocks, such as shown right, are one way to control mist systems. One clock turns the entire system ON in the morning and OFF at night. The other clock controls the frequency of misting. The third clock shown controls a supplementary light system.

This problem can be reduced by putting in a thermal layer of polyethylene film or insulating the windows on the outside at night to prevent the collision of warm and cold air. A small fan to keep the warm air circulating will also reduce condensation.

Mist Systems

If you are in an area where you have to fight high temperatures and low humidity much of the year, a misting system may be a good solution for your greenhouse. A mist system is also excellent for propagating new plants. It's a means of minimizing plant moisture loss and cutting greenhouse temperatures. But most importantly mist systems lower the leaf temperature and allow photosynthesis to continue at a good rate.

Mist systems are normally set up with two timers, one to turn the entire system on during the day and off at night, and another to run the spray nozzles a few seconds every few minutes. You should set the timing sequence yourself, based on what your plants need. Spray nozzles should be activated when the leaves are dried and should be on only long enough to thoroughly wet all the leaves. (This can be as much as 20 times an hour in very hot and dry areas.)

The problem with clock-type controls is they don't take into consideration the times when the sun is behind clouds and there is less evaporation from the leaves. This produces a tendency to overwater. Newer systems use a balance rod with a piece of screen on one end and the other end hooked to the on-off switch. When water builds up on the screen, as it would on a leaf, the rod dips and shuts off the misters; when the water has evaporated, it rises and switches the misters back on.

Misting does not promote diseases as you might suspect but actually retards some, such as powdery mildew.

Mist Propagation Bench

A mist propagation bench can be set up in any part of your greenhouse. The bench should be made of a material impervious to water, such as corrugated cement asbestos covered with 1 inch of gravel and topped with 2 inches of sand to provide quick drainage. This system is excellent for rooting cuttings in flats. If you want to root directly into the bench, you will need another 2 inches of soil mix on top. For best results, the growing medium should be warmed with electric cables since the misting tends to lower the soil temperatures.

To bring the water for misting to the bench, a ¾-inch PVC pipe is usually adequate. The pipe can either be suspended overhead or built into the bench with ½-inch PVC pipe risers. Either way, the spray nozzles should be about 18 inches above the cuttings.

The spacing of the misters will depend on their size and make. Follow the manufacturer's directions carefully. You want all areas of the bench covered, which means some overlap, but no excess.

If you are misting only in a small section of the greenhouse, you can hang curtains of clear plastic film around the misters to keep other areas dry.

Light

It can't be said too often that light—winter sunlight—must be the greatest concern of the greenhouse grower. No matter how well or how often we do the other things a plant needs, the short winter days will determine whether the poinsettias bloom for Christmas or the forced bulbs will bloom for Valentine's Day. It is light that will mainly determine whether you can have a zygocactus in bloom at Thanksgiving or a Christmas cactus. The pot mum that is made to bloom in June or July is responding to the controlled day length you maintain for it. Some plants are not very particular if they have long or short days or nights but some are going to be very particular as to when they bloom based on the amount of light they receive.

Greater amounts of light are usually necessary during the flowering or reproducing stage, as distinct from the negative period that each plant has in its annual cycle. A chrysanthemum that naturally blooms in the fall forms its buds in the late summer when the days are long and the nights are short. Therefore, if you want to grow it in the greenhouse so it will bloom in the spring or early summer, you must provide it with a relatively long period of light in the preceding months. You can do this in the greenhouse by using artificial light while shading the other plants that aren't in the same cycle.

The real fun of growing plants is in working with nature. Pretty soon it becomes natural to do so. If you can get yourself into this habit of looking at the natural cycle of a plant, you will learn to do for the plants what they need.

Soil and Water

The relationship between soil and water is so close that they should be talked about together. Early on in this book it was noted that the rate of a plant's photosynthesis and therefore growth depends on its having a constant supply of dissolved minerals and water being taken into the plant through the roots. If the plant can't get the minerals—either from the soil itself or added fertilizer—and there is not the proper amount of water, then growth will be stunted or stopped altogether.

Do You Need Special Soil Mix?

If you take the word of the most successful commercial growers of plants in containers, the answer is "yes."

If you take the word of the hundreds of thousands of home gardeners who have bought and used a container mix, again the answer is "yes." Garden stores everywhere sell special container mixes under a wide variety of trade names—Redi-Earth, Jiffy Mix, Metro Mix, Super Soil, Pro-Mix, Baccto, and many others.

The mixes are referred to as "soilless mixes" or "synthetic soils." The word synthetic should not be translated as "artificial."

The Basic Ingredients for Container Soils and Why.

The organic fraction of the mix may be peat moss, redwood sawdust, shavings, bark of hardwoods, fir bark, pine bark, or a combination of any two.

The mineral fraction may be vermiculite, perlite, pumice, builders sand or granite sand, or a combination of two or three of them. The most commonly used minerals are: vermiculite, perlite, and fine sand.

Vermiculite (Terralite) when mined resembles mica. Under heat treatment the mineral flakes expand with air spaces to 20 times their original thickness.

Perlite (Sponge rock) when mined is a granite-like volcanic material that when crushed and heat treated (1500°–2000° F) pops like popcorn and expands to 20 times its original volume.

The mix you buy may be 50% peat moss and 50% vermiculite, or 50% ground bark and 50% fine sand, or other combinations of the organic and mineral components. The ingredients in the mixes vary but the principle behind all mixes is the same: soilless "soil" must provide:

1. Fast drainage of water through the "soil."
2. Air in the "soil" after drainage.
3. A reservoir of water in the "soil" after drainage.

Most important in any container mix is "air in the soil" after drainage. Plant roots require air for growth

If You Want to Make Your Own Container Mix

If you are going at container gardening in a big way, with large containers for shrubs and trees, consider the following formulas.

But first consider the advantages of buying the prepared commercial mixes. What are you going to do with the mix?

Few home gardeners have need for large quantities of a mix designed for seedlings and small pots. And, when growing seedlings or growing seed in pots, sterilization of the growing medium is all important.

Top left, a typical commercially available potting soil. Surrounding it are some common ingredients of home-made mixes. Clockwise from top right: perlite, vermiculite, fir bark, peat moss, and coarse builders sand.

When the need for container "soil" is limited to a few cubic feet, the purchase of one of the commercial mixes is your best bet.

However, these are the components you would blend together for one yard of very lightweight mix for seedlings and pots:

- 9 cubic feet of peat moss
- 9 cubic feet of vermiculite
- 9 cubic feet of perlite
- 5 pounds of 5-10-10 fertilizer
- 5 pounds of ground limestone

For a slightly heavier mix for seedlings and pots:

- 7 cubic feet of fine sand
- 14 cubic feet of peat moss
- 7 cubic feet of perlite
- 5 pounds of 5-10-10 fertilizer
- 8 pounds of ground limestone

In all formulas we have substituted a fertilizer mix of 5-10-10 for combinations of super phosphate, calcium or potassium nitrate in the amounts called for in the Cornell Bulletin #43. Check the bulletin if you wish to duplicate their procedure in producing the Peat-Lite mixes.

A mix recommended for indoor foliage plants goes like this:

- 14 cubic feet of peat moss
- 7 cubic feet of vermiculite
- 7 cubic feet of perlite
- 5 pounds of 5-10-10 fertilizer
- 1 pound of iron sulphate
- 8 pounds of ground limestone

The proportions for a mix for most shrubs and trees:

- 9 cubic feet of fine sand
- 18 cubic feet of ground bark or nitrogen stabilized sawdust or

- 9 cubic feet of fine sand
- 9 cubic feet of peat moss
- 9 cubic feet of ground bark

add to either of the above:

- 5 pounds of 5-10-10 fertilizer
- 7 pounds of ground limestone
- 1 pound of iron sulphate

Can you convert your garden soil into a container soil?

The organic materials used in the commercial synthetic mixes are almost stabilized in their decomposition. Peat moss, redwood sawdust, fir bark, and pine bark, "stay put" in a container mix. We have plants in containers in which a mix of fir bark and sand has held up for five years.

In conditioning a garden soil, gardeners properly add all types of organic material—peat moss, ground bark, manure, leaf mold, and compost, in all stages of decay. All organic materials are beneficial in making heavy soils more friable and sandy soils more retentive of water and nutrients. If the manure and compost add to the fertility of the soil, so much the better. When using such organic amendments or organic mulches of leaves, straw, or grass clippings, it's common practice to add the organic matter to the soil every year to replace those that break down.

Materials that shrink or disappear do not belong in a container mix. A garden soil—clay loam or sandy loam—mixed with either peat moss, nitrogen stabilized sawdust, or ground bark, will give you the most satisfactory mix.

Watering

The watering of plants is probably the least understood and most mismanaged aspect of gardening. Water means many things to a plant. It is the solvent that carries the minerals from the soil through the plant; it is a raw material used by the plant in synthesizing other more complex compounds; it is an essential item in the process of photosynthesis for the production of food; and water cools the plant through transpiration into the air. Water is taken into a plant as a liquid through the root hairs, used by the plant, and given off into the atmosphere as a vapor.

The usual greenhouse plant has to grow in a very confined space and a limited amount of soil. To compensate for this, greenhouse plants must be assured of good drainage, a porous soil that will retain moisture, and then plenty of water. But whenever the plant is watered, some of the available nutrients are leached out of the pot or soil and should be replaced with a suitable fertilizer.

Be careful with thick, hairy-leaved plants such as the African violet (*Saintpaulia*). Water will cause spots on their leaves if the temperature of the water is not very close to that of the leaves. Such plants must be watered directly in the pot or from saucers of water under them.

Fertilizer—when and how much

When using a mix containing a 5-10-10 fertilizer, feeding normally should begin 3 weeks after planting. If frequent watering is necessary after planting start the feeding program earlier.

Because fertilizers are leached through the mixes when watered, the frequency of watering determines the frequency of fertilizing. Fertilizers will leach from mixtures containing perlite faster than from a mix containing vermiculite. Therefore, plants grown in a peat moss-perlite mix will require more frequent applications of fertilizer.

Some container gardeners prefer to fertilize with a weak nutrient solution, applying it with every other irrigation. When watering plants with a nutrient solution in this manner, a safe concentration would be 1/5 the amount called for on the label for a monthly application. If the label calls for 1 tablespoon to a gallon of water, make the dilution 1 tablespoon to 5 gallons of water.

Plants growing in containers demand closer attention than the same plants growing in a flower border or in a vegetable patch. When you constrict the root zone in a container you must compensate for the smaller root area by both more frequent watering and feedings.

The amount of fertilizer needed at any one time is very small but the need is continuous. The nutrient solution applications, as described above, satisfy the need for a constant supply of nutrients. The use of the time-release fertilizers is another popular method. The timing is taken care of by applying nutrients in a form that becomes available in small amounts as the plant is watered. Check the labels for rate of application. The use of a time-release fertilizer mixed with the soil just before planting is the easiest method to follow.

Let There Be Light

The effects of light-whether incandescent or fluorescent—and how to control them. How to build your own light garden.

Light is one of the most important elements necessary to healthy plant growth. It is the energizing force in the process all green plants use to make simple sugars from water and carbon dioxide. Without light and the green plants to trap its energy, life could not exist as we know it today.

This sugar producing process, *photosynthesis* (from *photo* = light and *synthesis* = to put together), is truly one of nature's miracles. It is a solar energy "trap" far more efficient than any yet devised by man.

This diagram shows where light fits in the process of photosynthesis:

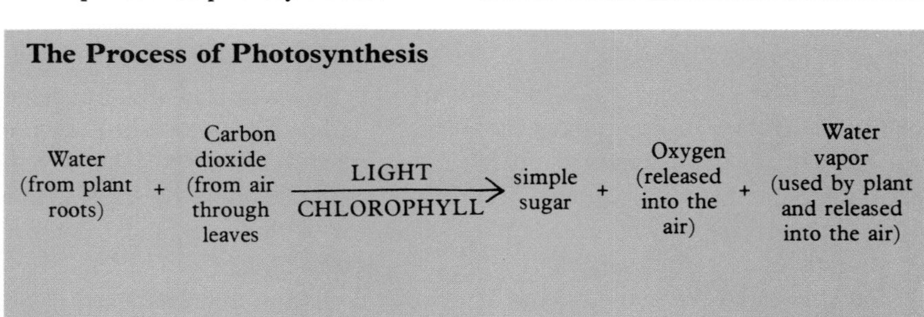

Light is radiant energy. Technically it is the visible portion of the electromagnetic wavelength spectrum.

Visible light is a blend of red, orange, yellow, green, blue and violet rays. Beyond the visible blue-violet are invisible ultra violet rays; at the other end of the spectrum, invisible infrared rays lie just beyond the visible red. Plants absorb primarily blue and red light and reflect green and yellow.

Blue and violet rays promote foliage growth. Plants grown with blue light alone tend to be compact and with lush, dark green leaves, but with few flowers. Red and far-red light affects several growth processes. Among them are the elongation and expansion of various plant parts and, notably, flowering. These effects have been identified by plant scientists although they've yet to discover how they occur. Research has not revealed any major effects of yellow or green rays on plant growth.

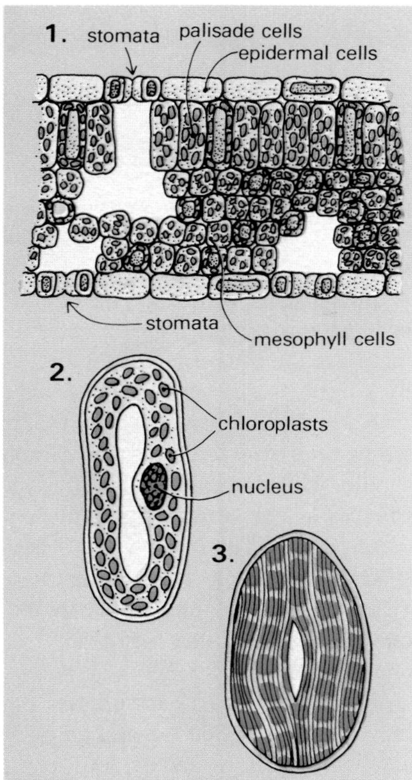

1. The cross-section of a leaf shows the water-proof upper and lower epidermal cells with stomata (pores) through which water vapor, oxygen, and carbon dioxide enter and leave the leaf; the layer of palisade cells, just below the upper surface, where most of the chloroplasts and therefore, most of the photosynthesis occurs; and the mesophyll cells where the products of photosynthesis are stored before transfer to other parts of the plant. **2.** A single palisade cell showing the nucleus and many chloroplasts. **3.** A single chloroplast with its grana, groups of minute plates called lamellae in which most of the chlorophyll molecules are found.

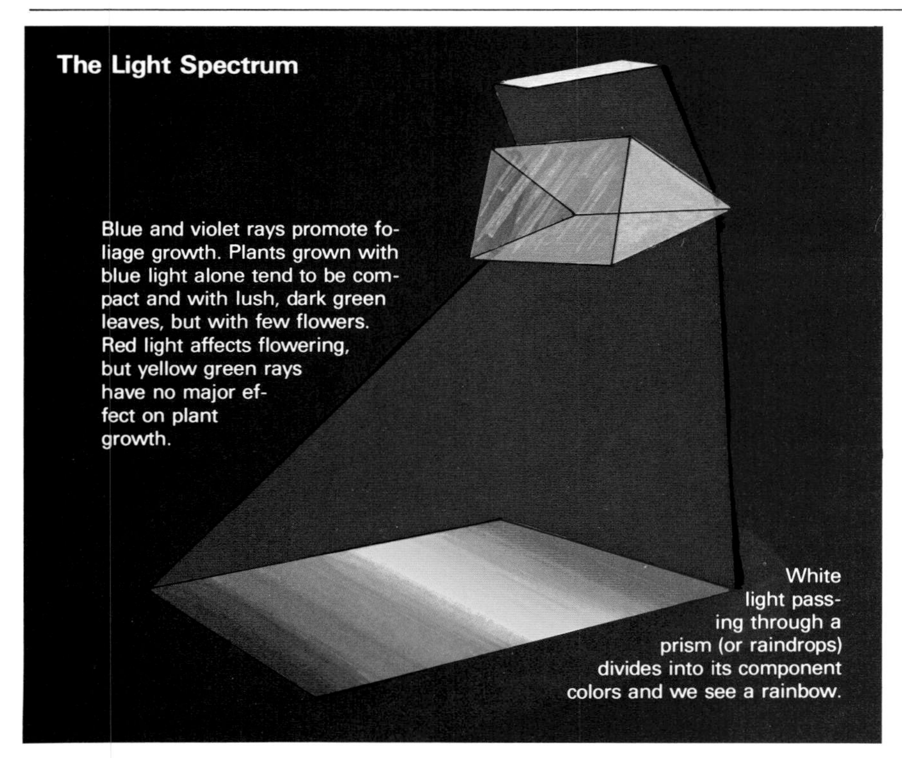

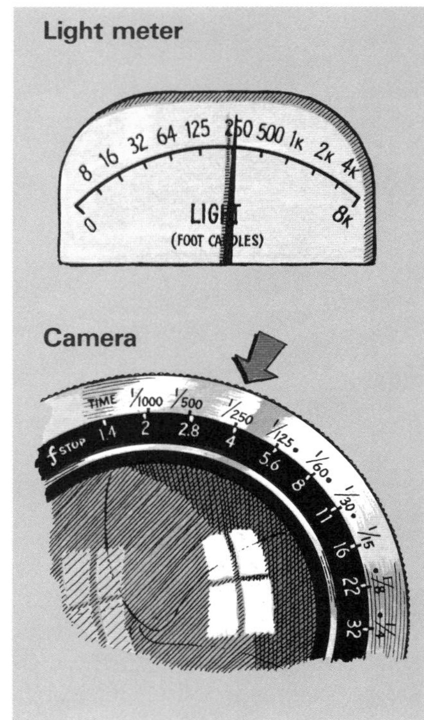

Measuring light

Light is measured in footcandles and lumens, depending on whether one is considering the object that is lighted or the source of the light.

Footcandles, or f.c., are the amount of light *received* on a surface, and lumens are the measure of light *emitted* by a light source.

Natural sunlight and artificial light falling on a plant are measured in footcandles while the light emitted by such sources as the sun itself and electric lamps are rated in lumens.

One footcandle is the amount of visible light falling on one square foot of surface located one foot away from one standard candle.

For example, a clear summer day may measure 10,000 f.c. and an overcast winter day as low as 500 f.c. To read comfortably requires about 20 f.c. The light of the full moon measures less than 1 f.c.

The most accurate way to estimate light is to use mechanical means. This can be done with a special light meter which reads directly in footcandles, or we can utilize a photographer's light meter or the light meter that is built into a camera and translate the photographic readings.

A light meter with a scale in direct footcandle readings is manufactured by the General Electric Company. It is Model #24 and can measure up to 10,000 footcandles.

This light meter measures the footcandles falling on a piggyback plant, (Tolmeia menziesii).

The proper way to make a reading is to place the meter at the same position as the surface of the leaves. Aim the plastic-covered lens toward the maximum light source. Without blocking the light or casting a shadow on the meter, check the reading on the dial.

A photographic meter or camera with a built-in light meter will provide fairly accurate readings that can be translated into footcandles. Here are two methods:

Method 1. Set the film-speed dial to ASA 100 and aim the camera or hand held meter at a sheet of matte white cardboard or paper in the proposed plant location and orient to the maximum light source. Get close enough to the paper so the meter sees only the white paper. Be sure not to block the light or create a shadow. The shutter speed indicated opposite stop f4, reading it as a whole number, will be the approximate footcandles of illumination measured. For example, if the f-stop registers an exposure of 1/250th second, there are about 250 f.c. of light playing on the white sheet.

Method 2. Set the ASA film-speed at 20 and the shutter speed at 1/125th second. Focus on the white paper as above. Adjust the f-stop until a correct exposure is shown in the light meter in the camera. By using the table below, the f-stop will tell you how many footcandles you have.

f2.8	32f.c.
f4	64f.c.
f5.6	125f.c.
f8	250f.c.
f11	500f.c.
f16	1000f.c.
f22	2000f.c.

The camera's photographic meter measures the same spectrum of visible light as the footcandle meter. The latter registers intermediate readings and is more accurate as well.

Growth chambers allow plant scientists to control light. Duration, intensity, and quality of light can be manipulated.

Effects of Light

The effects of light on plants are many and varied. Its most important qualities are its intensity and duration. Measuring the light as described above is a guide to intensity.

Generally a plant surviving at low light intensities only *maintains* itself; if it receives more light, it *grows.* When intensity dips below the minimum a plant can tolerate, it slowly weakens and dies. A plant in this state may appear healthy for some months, but in fact it is living on stored energy and is slowly declining.

Scientists use the word *etiolation* to describe plants grown in very low light or darkness. It is a French word meaning "to blanch." Etiolated plants are typically spindly and actually grow taller than if in adequate light. The color is pale and leaves are poorly developed. Many gardeners' introduction to etiolation is seedlings that quickly grow tall then fall of their own weight—such seedlings are grown in light levels that are low.

Plants exposed to light intensities too high exhibit variable symptoms. Leaves may wilt during the hottest part of the day, curl downward and develop brown, burned spots. The foliage may undergo color change. Lush greens may bleach to unhealthy yellow. Beyond color change is outright leafburn. For instance, orchids exposed to excessive light intensity will develop blackened areas on the leaves.

Plants should never be subjected to drastic change of light without conditioning. A plant adapted to shade conditions can suffer fatal burning when moved to a sunny location that it possibly, with conditioning, could tolerate. The results can be compared to a person, pale from winter indoors, going to the beach and getting severely burned by spending too many hours in the sun. Many plants that could become accustomed to low light levels die when shifted from an area of much higher light.

Photoperiodism. All plants are light-programmed to their own native environment and perform best in the rhythmic light/darkness cycle found there. For many plants the length of nights and days is a determining factor in the time required to reach maturity —that stage in a plant's life when reproduction becomes possible.

Some plants flower when the days are long and the nights short; these are called *long-day* plants. Some long-day plants are calceolaria, tuberous begonia, cineraria, bromeliads, azalea, coleus, gloxinia, stephanotis, and African violets.

Conversely, other plants produce blooms when days are short and nights long; these are the *short-day* plants. Common short-day plants are gardenias, kalanchoe, chrysanthemum, Christmas cactus, poinsettia, cattleya orchids, aphelandra, and fuchsia.

Many plants however have no definite response—they are *day-neutral.* They bloom with varying hours of light.

Armed with this knowledge, plants can be brought into bloom any time of year. Supplement light to long-day plants with artificial lights. Short-day plants requiring twelve hours or more of darkness can be shaded with black cloth before natural day ends. Shading must be complete. Tiny quantities of light leaking through will prevent flowering.

Artificial light

Artificial lights have by many times expanded the flexibility and capability of gardeners. Plants can grow and bloom in a situation where artificial light is the sole energy source. Or, more naturally, artificial light can be used to supplement sunlight.

Incandescent light

These are the common light bulbs used every day in the home. They consist of a tungsten filament wire which has high resistance to electricity. The resistance caused by the filament re-

Lengthen nights artificially and chrysanthemums will flower anytime.

Incandescent "plant growth" lamps provide main light source for a corner bedroom garden of foliage plants.

sults in the emission of visible light.

This is a light source rich in red and far-red light which is necessary for flowering and other plant processes. In fact, incandescent light possesses the same proportion of these colors as sunlight, although vastly less intense. However the total energy output is insufficient among the blue and violet rays of the spectrum and therefore the incandescent light as a sole energy source is not suitable for complete plant growth.

Incandescents also give off a considerable amount of heat. This of course can damage plants growing too close. Generally keep the tops of plants at least a foot away from incandescent sources. However, if your hand feels warm when held at the foliage closest to the light source, the plant is too close.

The lamp should not be placed too far away from the plant either. The light reaching the plant will decrease with the square of the distance that it is removed. That is, a plant two feet away from a light source will receive only one-fourth as much light as it would if it were one foot away.

Probably the easiest way to reduce heat of incandescent bulbs is to use 130 volt types. These are "industrial" grade—they burn cooler and longer than standard 120 volt bulbs.

Another way to reduce incandescent heat is to utilize several smaller bulbs instead of fewer larger ones. This distributes the heat over a large area, allows placing the lamps closer to the plants, and provides more even distribution of light.

A third method of avoiding heat problems is to use reflectorized incandescent lamps. These have names such as Cool Beam or Cool Lux. They contain a reflecting surface which allows light to pass but directs heat upward. Use a heavy duty ceramic socket with these bulbs.

Probably the most involved but most reliable way to reduce heat is a shield of glass or transparent plastic between the lights and the plants. This will absorb or reflect a large amount of heat while allowing nearly all of the light to pass through to the plant. The shield should be placed several inches away from the lamp.

Fluorescent Light

Fluorescent lamps supply the light most gardeners choose. They are more efficient, supplying 2½ to 3 times as much light and only a fraction the heat of an incandescent bulb of the same wattage. Also the lifetime of a fluorescent tube is 15 to 20 times that of an incandescent.

The glass tube of a fluorescent lamp is coated on the inside with a phosphor. It is the type of phosphor that determines the "color" of the light given off. Mixing various phosphors determines the "mix" of the various color wavelengths. The visible color of the light emitted, however, is not indicative of the proportion of blue and red waves given off. Remember that plants do not "see" light as we do.

The bulb also contains a blend of inert gasses such as argon, neon, or krypton, and a minute quantity of mercury vapor, sealed in low pressure. Electricity causes a current to flow between the electrodes at each end of the tube. This current is in the form of an electrical arc which stimulates the phosphor coating and emits energy in the form of light.

Although initially more expensive than incandescent bulbs, fluorescent lamps form the backbone of light gardening. They can be positioned as close as one inch to many blooming plants,

Two styles of light gardens on wheels: Top, ceiling suspended lights; a work bench on wheels. Above, completely portable, self-contained unit.

although six to nine inches is more common. They should not be placed more than 18 inches away from the top of a plant unless the lamps are high output.

The high-output tubes are the type of lamp used by scientists and advanced light gardeners. Their higher intensity permits greater tube-to-plant distances as well as allowing greatest possible flexibility for successful artificial light gardening. These tubes are available from all the major electric companies.

We've described how to measure light to be sure of adequate intensity for plant growth. Using fluorescent

The trough is filled with water and the capillary mat pulls the water by "wick" action, maintaining even moisture beneath each pot.

light, there is another way to figure how much light to provide: total wattage per square foot. Experience indicates that about 20 watts per square foot is adequate for plants normally requiring low light levels, and 40 watts per square foot for high light plants. Of course, intensity can be further manipulated by adjusting the distance between the lights and the plants.

Most light gardeners leave lights on for as few as 10 and as many as 18 hours a day. With foliage plants it makes little difference. However, most plants that flower have more specific needs. Learn about the plants you desire to grow.

Fluorescents, like incandescents, "blacken" with age and lose light efficiency. Therefore for best plant growth, it is recommended they be replaced when they reach 70% of their stated service life. By that time, they'll be delivering about 15% less light than when new.

Another artificial light source has recently become available. It is marketed under the name "Wonderlite." Wonderlite is newsworthy because it provides the growth promoting effects of fluorescent lamps without the necessity of special fixtures—it threads into normal light bulb sockets. With Wonderlite alone, flowering plants can be brought into bloom.

Plant "Grow Lamps"

These are sold under the names of Gro-Lux, Vita-lite, Agro-lite, and Naturescent/Optima among others. They are of two types: 1) "wide spectrum" in which the visual qualities of sunlight are duplicated; and 2) "spectrum enhanced" in which the rays known to be most important to plant growth are maximized.

The wide spectrum lamps include the visible blue and far-red rays, and sometimes the ultra-violet rays as well. Their light has a "daylight" quality. They do not only aid plant growth, but provide a more realistic visual rendition of plant color than the grow lights. Due to the added far-red in wide spectrum bulbs, which is not visible, the light given off is reduced compared to standard cool or warm white.

The spectrum enhanced lamps are coated with special phosphors that reduce the green/yellow rays that are of little value to plants. The lamp's energy is concentrated on the blue/red parts of the spectrum. Because of the missing values the light given out tends to be purplish or pinkish.

The plastic sheet helps maintain humidity and temperature. Incandescent bulbs add "red" light important to flowering plants.

Fluorescent and Incandescent Combined

Ordinary fluorescent light in the right intensities can promote lush foliage growth, even bring some plants to flower. Like incandescent, it is short on certain parts of the spectrum. All common fluorescent output is very high in the blue light, which in general promotes foliage growth, and low in red and far-red important in the flowering process.

Many artificial light gardeners claim the best solution to this dilemma is to combine fluorescent and incandescent. Usually talk is in terms of ratios of watts.

However, we found so many varying ratios suggested that it is difficult to do more than report them. The quantity of fluorescent light is always greater. Anywhere between 1:2 and 1:5 has been recommended by various gardeners. In other words, 200 or 500 watts of fluorescent light to 100 watts incandescent. Another approach suggests 1:3 for wattages below 1,000 f.c. increasing it to 1:2 above 2,000 f.c.

The researchers of the United States Department of Agriculture Experimental Station in Beltsville, Maryland, have long studied the relationship of light quality to plant growth. Recently, two scientists working there, H. Marc Cathey and L. E. Campbell, summarized their research regarding the effects of light sources on plant growth.

Fluorescent (cool white and warm white)

- Green foliage that expands to parallel to the surface of the lamp
- Stems elongate slowly
- Multiple side shoots develop
- Flowering occurs over a long period of time

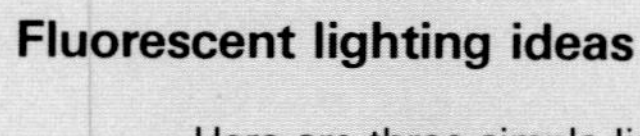

Fluorescent lighting ideas

Here are three simple light gardens to alter "daylength" or start seedlings. The fluorescent fixture on the adjustable shelf brackets can be moved up or down to give your plants more or less light.

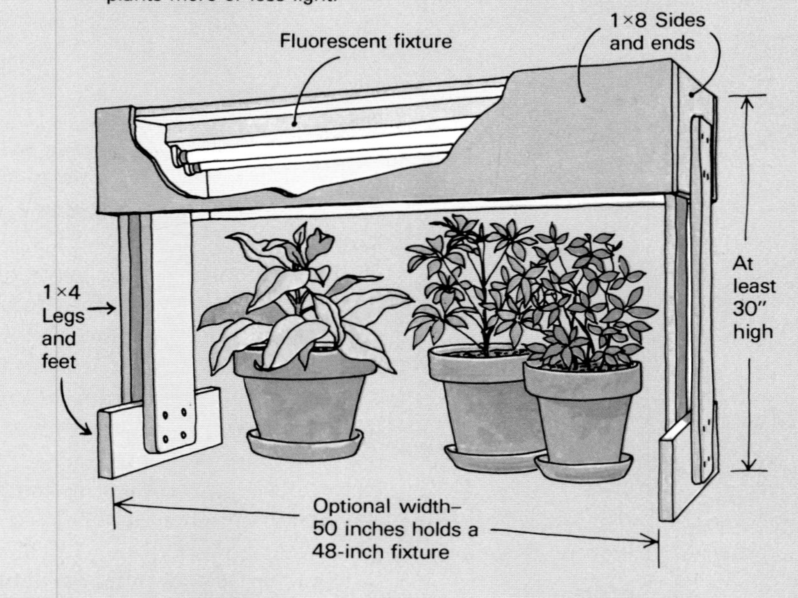

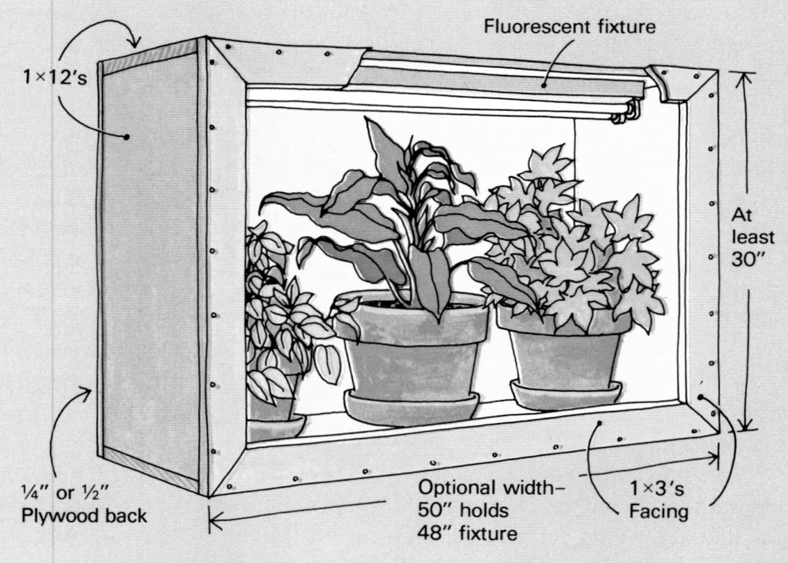

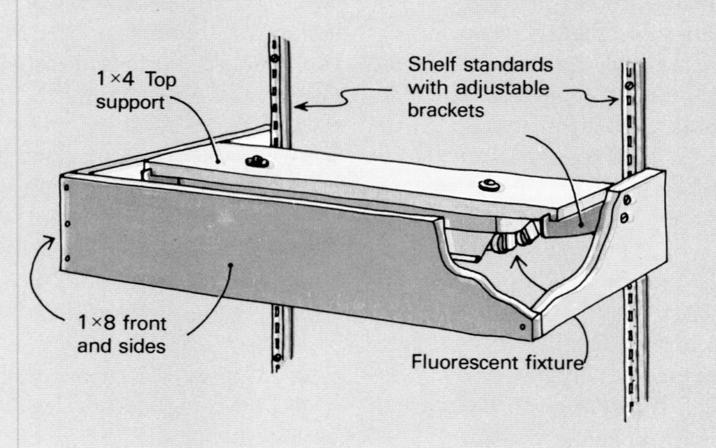

Fluorescent, enhanced spectrum (Gro-Lux)

■ Deep green foliage that expands, often larger than on plants grown under cool white or warm white

■ Stems elongate slowly, extra thick stems develop

■ Multiple side shoots develop

■ Flowering occurs late, flower stalks do not elongate

Fluorescent, wide spectrum (Vita-lite, Agro-lite, and others)

■ Light green foliage that tends to ascend toward the lamp

■ Stems elongate rapidly

■ Suppresses development of multiple side shoots

■ Flowering occurs soon, flower stalks elongated, plants mature and age rapidly

Incandescent

■ Paling of foliage, thinner and longer than on plants grown under other light sources

■ Stem elongation is excessive, eventually becomes spindly and easily breaks

■ Side shoot development is suppressed, plants expand only in height

■ Flowering occurs rapidly, plants mature and become senescent quickly

Building Artificial Light Gardens

Under cupboards. There's a good place for lights in many homes: under kitchen cupboards. You might find that a splash of colorful plants there year-round is restful on the eyes. In this kitchen (see photographs), two 40 watt bulbs were placed under a cabinet. Small staples held the cords out of the way. The lights however were visible when sitting at the nearby dining table and cast an uncomfortable glare. To hide them, a 1×4 board was screwed to a 2×2 and cut off to fit under the counter. In place, it shielded the glaring lights.

Windows

If you have a kitchen window that faces north and receives little light, or a bathroom window in your apartment that receives almost no light, brighten them with overhead lights. The combination of lights and plants can dramatically change the room's appearance.

If you have wooden window sills, you can screw the fluorescent light directly to the underside of the frame. If you don't already have a valance up there to shield the light, you will have to put some other protection there. Experiment with a strip of cardboard to find how deep the protective shield must be so the light is not easily seen. If 8 inches provides good shielding, for instance, then cut a 1×8 board the width of your window, paint it to match and screw it in place.

If you can't hang that light inside the window, then use this shelf bracket method. Screw short lengths of heavy duty shelf standards to either side of the window frame at the top. Then, using brackets at least 2 inches longer than your light fixture is wide, bolt 1×8 boards to the outside of the brackets. Use glue and 6d finishing nails to put on the 1×8 front piece that will shield the light. Across the top, nail a 1×4 down the middle and hang the light from that. When all assembled and painted, hang it from the shelf standards. This should provide ample support but for windows wider than 4 feet, use a center support.

You can use this same shelf system to make a light garden that will grow with the plants. The lights may start 2 inches above a seedling bed but as the plants grow the lights have got to be raised to keep pace. This is particularly useful when starting tomatoes indoors in anticipation of transplanting outdoors for early production.

Table Top Units

These are both useful and attractive on narrow tables in long, dim hallways. Since fluorescent lights and fixtures come in a great variety of lengths, they will fit over almost any table.

For a simple but effective table top model, start by constructing a three-sided box. It can be up to 8 feet long with no center supports. Use a 1×2 for the top and 1×6 for the sides. If you can, miter all the joints at a 45 degree angle for a smoothly finished exterior with no end wood showing. Paint the inside of the box white for added reflection and then screw the light fixture to the inside top of the box.

For the supporting legs, use four 1×4s cut 8 inches long. Round one end on each leg, using a coffee can or small plate as a guide. Bolt two legs together over each end of the box, clasping the 1×6 end pieces. The feet of the legs are made by clasping and bolting an 11-inch length of 1×4.

Instead of using decorative bolts, you can use wood screws, countersinking them all and either filling with wood putty or filling the holes with small wooden buttons designed for that purpose.

Cabinet Light Garden

A dramatic light garden for that dark side of the room is made by constructing a basic cabinet frame. It's really nothing more than a large box on its side with the front open. It can double as a bookcase also. The dimensions given here can be altered to fit your needs.

Using 1×12 wood that is kiln or air dried so it will not warp, cut the two end pieces 3 feet 10 inches long and the top and bottom pieces each 6 feet long. Miter the ends if you have the tools, otherwise use butt joints. Use white glue and 6d nails to put the frame together. Cut a piece of ½-inch plywood to 4×6 feet and glue and nail to the back of the frame.

Inside each end piece drill a parallel row of holes 4 inches apart for the metal shelf holders. Cut two shelves 5 feet 10½ inches long from 1×12.

Now, to hide the fixtures and give the cabinet a finished appearance, face all the outside edges with 1×4, including the shelves. Miter the corners of the edging on the cabinet frame to fit together at a 45 degree angle. Paint the interior and the underside of each shelf white to give added reflection. The tops of the shelves on the cabinet can be painted to match your decor. Fasten the fluorescent fixtures under the top and the two shelves and then place your plants. Putting the plants on pebble trays would help increase humidity if necessary.

Vertical Light Box

Not all plants are small by any means and the tall ones need as much or more light when growing indoors. If you have a 6-foot tall philodendron in need of light, try this vertical light box.

Cut two 1×8 long forms in the back. It is centered 4 inches from the top and bottom. Use white glue and 6d nails to put the back between the two sides, setting it in 2 inches. Cut two pieces of 1×6 each 3½ inches long to enclose the lights at the top and bottom. Paint the interior white and the outer edges a bright glossy color for contrast. Finish the sides to match your room decor.

To hold the light box firmly in place when vertical, attach a spring loaded pole to the back of the box with two pipe clamps.

Basement Gardens

If you have a little-used basement in your house, consider turning it into a major light garden.

To start this, build a series of shelves along one wall, running them from the floor to the ceiling. If you have an unfinished basement, you can nail vertical 2×4 supports right to the floor joists overhead. Or use 2×4 posts for the uprights and tie them together all around with 1×4s. Make each shelf section 3 feet wide and up to 8 feet long. Use ½-inch plywood for the shelves.

Mrs. Edna Oechesner of Roslyn, Long Island, New York, estimates she has 200 varieties of African violets in her basement fluorescent light garden. Watering is by capillary pad.

Solar Greenhouses & Sun Pits

Here are the basics on solar greenhouses and sun pits. How to build and use an attached or angled-wall solar greenhouse or sun pit.

If you've had second thoughts about starting a greenhouse because of the cost of heating it, then consider the solar greenhouse. The same applies if you already have a greenhouse. There are several ways to cut the heating bill, not only for the greenhouse but your own house as well.

Calling a greenhouse solar is somewhat redundant. More accurately, it should be termed a greenhouse with a solar heat sink. The greenhouse itself traps the heat each day, as anyone knows who has been in a greenhouse for just a few minutes on a sunny day, regardless of the outside temperature. But the greenhouse can't retain that heat by itself. To do this, it requires something for the heat to sink into and be stored—a mass, whether it be barrels of water, piles of rock or a pumice block wall that has been poured completely full of concrete.

Objects with considerable mass serve two purposes: During the day they soak up the heat, including some of the excess that would otherwise overheat your greenhouse. At night, this stored heat emanates back through the greenhouse. The success of this principle is just short of phenomenal. A case in point is a redwood and glass greenhouse in Santa Fe, New Mexico. At an altitude of 7,000 feet, Santa Fe has frigid winters and considerable snow, yet no outside source of heat was required in this greenhouse which has a 14-foot long, 8-foot high pumice block wall poured full of concrete as the heat sink. The lowest nighttime greenhouse temperature recorded was 42° F (5.5° C) when it was 4° F (−15° C) outside. During the day, heat from the greenhouse was pumped into the residence to help reduce the fuel bill.

There are two types of solar energy systems: active and passive. The most widely used in home greenhouses is the passive system where thermal mass, such as rocks or water-filled drums, is heated during the day and then radiate this heat back at night.

The active system requires electricity to pump heated air into a storage area, such as a basement, that is filled with rocks or water drums. It is a more efficient system than the passive, but also more costly and complex.

Solar Heat Storage

Heat arrives from the sun in the form of short waves, which strike and heat objects in the greenhouse. The heated objects radiate warmth back into the greenhouse in the form of long waves which do not readily penetrate the greenhouse covering. These long waves are the ones that can be trapped and stored. Thus, whatever style of greenhouse you have, or want, plan on using solar heat storage principles to cut your heating costs.

Opposite and right, greenhouse uses black, water-filled barrels to moderate temperatures. In winter, because of sun's low angle, barrels are warmed by sun's direct rays. Barrels are not reached (and not warmed) by rays of summer sun—they have cooling effect.

Solar heat sinks

Here are several materials and methods used for solar heat storage in greenhouses as well as other solar heating applications. See the text for specific recommendations and some construction details.

Stacked water-filled steel drum.

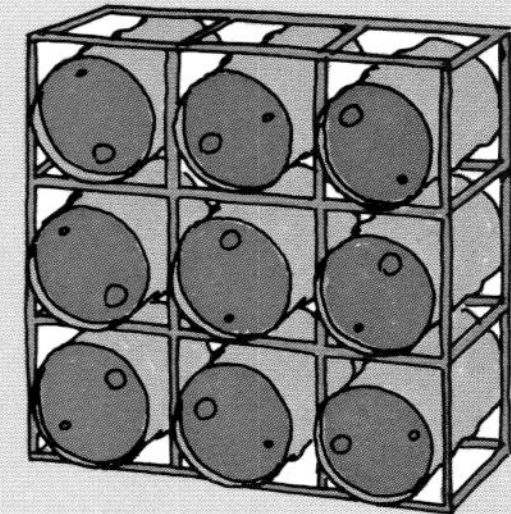

Water-filled steel drums on metal racks

Water-filled plastic containers on shelves.

Commercially made water-filled metal or plastic cylinders

Water-filled vinyl bags in concrete block cavities

Concrete-filled cinder or pumice concrete blocks

Brick, stone or adobe wall.

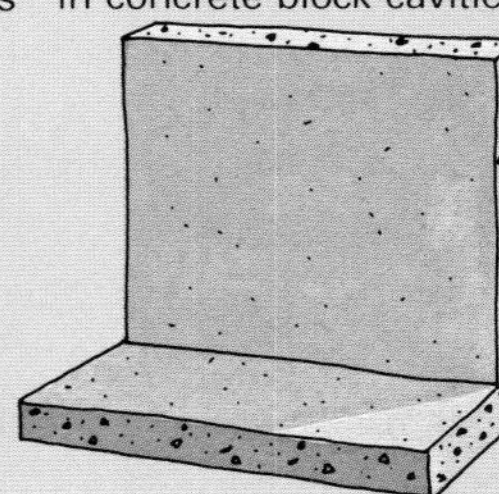

Concrete wall or slab floor

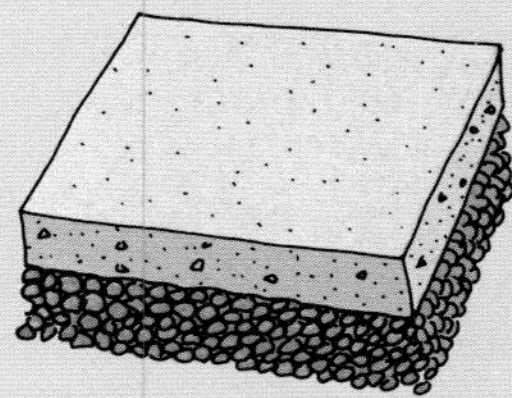

Concrete slab with bed of rocks beneath it

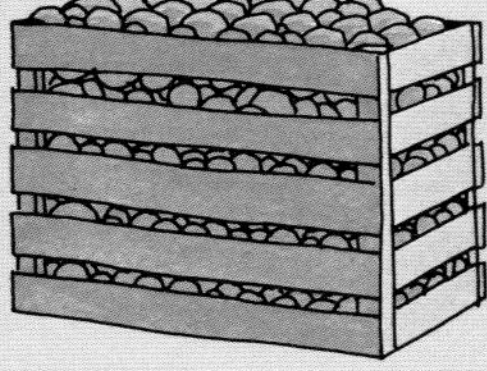

Bin (or loose pile) of rocks

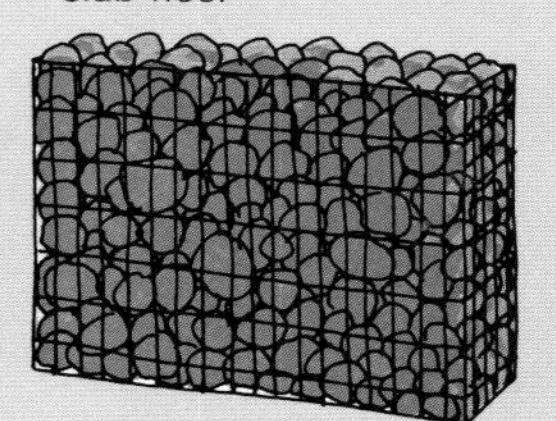

Rock wall held in place with wire mesh fencing

Passive system

The sun's warmth is deposited and held in the thermal-mass heat sink (in this case concrete-filled cinder blocks of the north wall and the brick floor) during the day. At night this heat radiates back out of the heat sink and keeps the area warm.

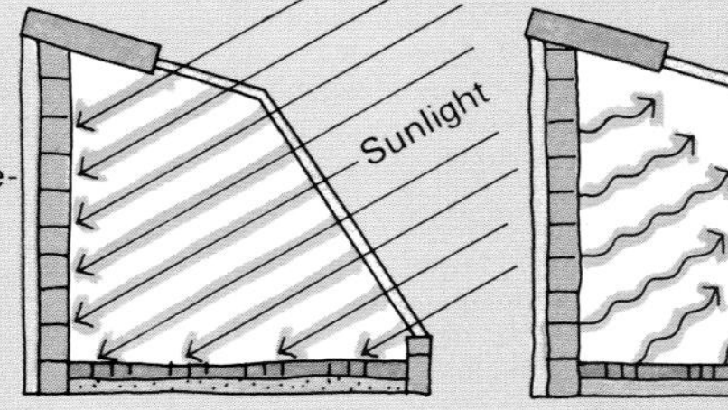

Active system

The sun's heat warms the transfer fluid (water or air) in a solar collector. This fluid is pumped to another location, such as the basement, and stored in a thermal mass heat sink. Another pump moves this heat again, as warm air, when its needed.

Probably the most widely used heat sink is water in a common 55-gallon drum with the drum painted a dark color to better absorb heat. Piles of rock are also widely used. We've found water to be much more efficient. Ten cubic feet of water—which is about a third as much again as 55 gallons—can store up to 18,700 Btu when the surrounding air temperture rises by 30° F (or about 17° C). The same amount of rock stores only 11,100 Btu, about 40 percent less than the water.

Whatever type of heat sink you choose to try, you cannot count on it to eliminate artificial heating totally unless your greenhouse can operate under ideal conditions. You need a backup unit ready, but you may find yourself not using it very often.

To calculate the minimum heat storage capabilities required, allow 2 gallons of water or 80 pounds of rock for each square foot of greenhouse that admits sunlight directly onto the storage units. Generally, just calculate the south-facing roof and wall. As an example, if the combined area of that roof and wall is a total of 200 square feet, you should have 400 gallons of water or 16,000 pounds of rock for an effective heat sink.

Drums can be bought for under $20 at most wholesale gasoline distributors. You can probably find them much cheaper by watching the want ads. Put the drums in place where they will collect the most heat and then fill with water. Leave three or four inches of room at the top to allow for expansion. Space the drums slightly to allow air to circulate around them freely. If you don't want black drums, paint them dark brown or green, but always use a flat nonreflective paint.

One caution here: Do not let the barrels touch any exterior wall or glazing. Remember that heat moves to cold and if barrels touch some glazing, the outside cold will quickly pull the heat from the barrel.

If you decide to use rocks instead of barrels, use chicken wire cages to hold the rocks. And again, remember that it requires mass to hold heat effectively, so the larger the rocks, the better the storage. Place them like the barrels, wherever they will receive maximum sunlight. Spray them a dark color unless they are naturally so already.

Some greenhouse gardeners use discarded plastic milk jugs set along the back of the bench to soak up heat. Although not efficient in small numbers, every little bit helps. It's a good way to warm the water for your plants instead of running a hot water line into the greenhouse.

Another efficient heat sink is either a brick wall or cinder blocks poured full of concrete. In the first instance, if you already have a lean-to greenhouse against your own house, cover your back wall with bricks. Buy black bricks or paint them dark for maximum heat absorption. Firmly affix this brick facing to the side of the house with steel braces set in the mortar and screwed to the house studs at regular intervals. It would be agony, not to mention messy, should that wall topple over after it was completed.

If you are going to build your own greenhouse, consider making a lean-to style with the north wall of pumice or cinder blocks poured full of concrete. When the outside of this wall is heavily insulated to prevent any heat loss, it becomes a highly effective heat sink, as proven in the Santa Fe greenhouse described later in detail.

The Solar Heated Greenhouse/Residence

The combination of a solar greenhouse with the living area is a high energy efficient system many have experimented with. Greenhouses are heat collectors while homes are heat users. The combination of the two makes good sense. Here are two examples of greenhouse/residence combinations. They store the heat trapped by the greenhouse during the day to warm both the greenhouse and the home during the night. Both heat *air* in collectors, then duct it to rockbeds for storage. Both use the energy of the sun twice—to grow plants and provide heat.

We visited the Environmental Research Laboratory at the University of Arizona. Solar engineer Dr. John Peck and research horticulturist Dr. Merle Jensen have developed a home solar collector that doubles as a year-round vegetable garden.

The entire south wall serves as the collector. It consists of two layers of thermal pane glass (usually 6 inches apart) with venetian blinds in between. The blinds are coated on one side with dark, heat absorbing paint. Sunlight heats the metal blinds which heat the air.

Their patented "ClearView" collector provides a virtually unobstructed view even when adjusted to collect heat. At night, they can be closed for privacy and to reduce heat loss. These collectors absorb 650 to 700 Btu's per square foot per day.

The rockbed used for heat storage has a 300-cubic foot capacity, and is filled with 3- to 6-inch rock. Air is circulated through the rock bed (and entire system) at about 60 feet per minute. To make use of the heat at night, the direction of air flow is reversed.

Still in development at ERL is a method of insulation using foam. In conjunction with double layer polyethylene, it can reduce heat loss up to 70%. Photographs on page 57 show the foam being injected. The foam lasts a few hours, becomes a liquid again, is collected and reused.

The greenhouse/residence is cooled by an evaporation-type cooler. When humidity is high, the rock bed is precooled at night. Air drawn through the rockbed the next day is cool and not humid. Precooled air from the rockbed can be further cooled by evaporation. Experimenting with such a system—dubbed "two-stage cooling," Peck and Jensen cooled air an additional 5 degrees. Where high humidity prevents effective use of evaporation cooling,

Scientists are exploring the possibilities of using an attached greenhouse as a heat source for a home. Such a system is in operation at the Environmental Research Laboratory of the University of Arizona.

Dr. Jensen suggests a partition between the growing and the living area and the use of refrigeration-type air-conditioning for the latter.

A wide variety of edible plants have been grown. Lettuce, other leafy vegetables, and herbs, are grown at ground level. Fruiting vegetables are grown in hanging pots near the roof of the chamber.

Fruiting plants such as tomato, eggplant, pepper, and cucumber require at least 6 hours of direct sunlight. Bananas of the dwarf 'Cavendish' type have been grown as well as the low growing 'Solo' papaya. A peat moss-vermiculite type soil mix is used; fertilizer is slow release; and irrigation is by a drip system. Yields have averaged over 2 pounds of vegetables per day since first planted in 1976.

Another combined greenhouse/solar collector system is designed by and installed at the home of Professor Edgar J. Carnegie of Morro Bay, California.

The system consists of a south facing, single flat plate solar collector 4 feet wide and 38 feet long. The collector is mounted flat on the edge of the roof.

Outside air is preheated 10 to 20 degrees by traveling through the greenhouse. It is then sucked into the solar collector inlet and further heated. From there, it moves through an 8-inch, insulated duct to the rock storage area.

The rockbed used for heat storage is 300 cubic feet in volume and filled with ¾-inch crushed gravel. Professor Carnegie figures these rocks, heated to 140°F. contain approximately 1,400 Btu's per cubic foot. In practice, this is enough to maintain the greenhouse area at a 55°F. minimum and still provide about 20 percent of his home heating needs.

A variety of plants are grown in his greenhouse, both ornamental and edible. He can grow tomatoes year round. The system is automated by use of thermostats and drip irrigation. The system cost $2,600.

Vegetables grown in the solar greenhouse include tomatoes (top), and Crowder peas

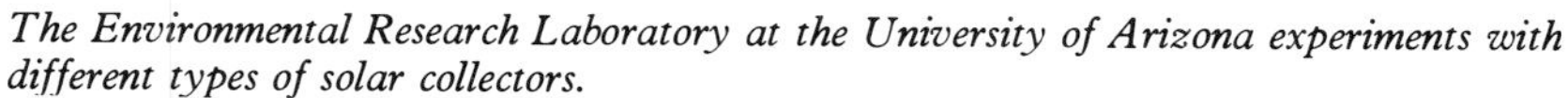

The Environmental Research Laboratory at the University of Arizona experiments with different types of solar collectors.

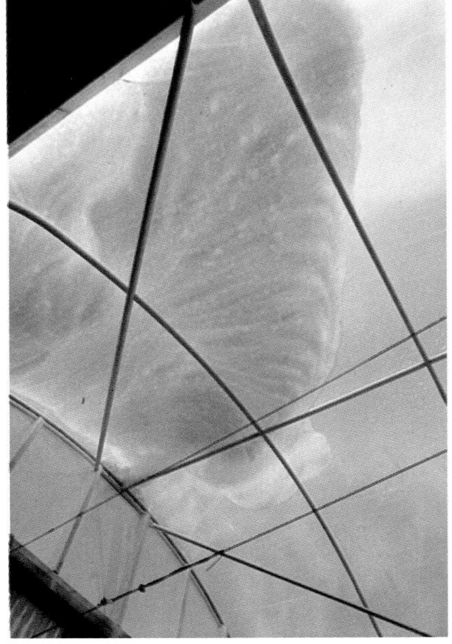

Insulation

All the heat you hope to store in your greenhouse will be lost if you can't prevent that heat from escaping as soon as it is radiated from the heat sink. The first and critically important task is to insure the greenhouse is as airtight as possible. Put weather stripping around the door and vents and use a flexible sealant to close all joints between the roof and walls. Double-check that all the glazing is in snugly. One little draft in a greenhouse will render the heat sink almost useless.

Even in a tightly sealed greenhouse, heat will continue to be lost through the glazing material. The quickest way to cut this loss is by stapling 4 mil polyethylene plastic around the inside of the greenhouse. (If it's a type that's ultraviolet-resistant it will last much longer.) Held at least an inch away from the wall, it can reduce heat losses by 30 to 40 percent, while cutting light reception by only about 10 percent.

When stretching the film, staple one end to a stick the same width as the plastic for a smooth, even pull. Don't stretch it too tightly because the plastic expands and contracts with temperature changes. In wood-framed greenhouses, staple over heavy twine. This serves both to prevent the staple from cutting through the plastic and to make it easy to remove the staples just by pulling the twine. Also, be careful to seal the bottom of the plastic film tightly against the bottom wall plate. If you don't, a chimney effect of air being drawn up through the gap will rapidly cool the greenhouse. If you have an aluminum greenhouse, several manufacturers now have reusable clips for putting up the polyethylene.

Greenhouse glazing can also be covered with plastic bubble pack. Some varieties are practically self-adhesive. Apply them by simply wetting—it will stick with hundreds of tiny suction cups. Other types of bubble pack may require 2-sided tape or spray-type adhesive to be secure against the glazing.

An effective but more time-consuming method of insulating is to cut pieces of rigid inch-thick insulation material, such as styrofoam or urethane, to fit each panel of glazing. Use small magnets and pieces of metal glued to the corners to fasten them in place. Where to store the insulation pieces during the day can be a problem but if they are white, they will help reflect more light around the greenhouse.

Reflection in the greenhouse is an important compromise with some solar heat storage principles. It takes a dark color to trap the heat rapidly, but that can result in phototropism problems, with the plants leaning away from the darkness toward the windows. You can help counter this by placing reflective material strategically.

Here, liquid foam is used for insulation. Still experimental, 70% reduction in heat loss is calculated.

An attached greenhouse-solar collector designed and built by Professor Edgar J. Carnegie of Morro Bay, California. Heat from the greenhouse is used to warm rocks. When necessary, heat is ducted from the rock storage into the home.

Reflection Capabilities

Material	*Percent of reflection*
White plaster	90–92%
Mirrored glass	80–90
Matte white paint	75–90
Porcelain enamel	60–90
Polished aluminum	60–70
Aluminum paint	60–70
Stainless steel	55–65

Insulated plywood panels on the outside walls of the greenhouse can help insulate it. During the day they are lowered by a pulley system and angled to reflect the maximum sunlight into the greenhouse. At night they are raised to cover the walls. But great care must be taken with this and similar reflected-light arrangements to avoid overheating the plants in the greenhouse.

The North Wall

The north wall of a greenhouse is the great escape route for both heat and light. Heat gained in the greenhouse where the sun comes through the glass is simply flowing out that north wall. In addition, light is being reflected out it and wasted. Some studies show that a conventional glass wall may have up to 15 times the heat loss of a conventional frame wall with 4 inches of fiberglass insulation.

If you already have a greenhouse, you can improve its performance by covering the north wall with a material that will both insulate and reflect light back into the interior. For an aluminum and glass structure, one effective method is to seal the north wall with panels of white, rigid insulation cut to fit each opening.

If you have a frame greenhouse, fill the north wall with batts of fiberglass insulation and then cover it with exterior grade plywood. First, apply a coat of water seal and then paint it white. With this additional light being bounced back, the north bench in the greenhouse can lose its reputation as a poor propagation area and become the best.

Two views inside the greenhouse of Professor Carnegie: facing west (above) and east (left). Note the exhaust fan and polyethylene glazing.

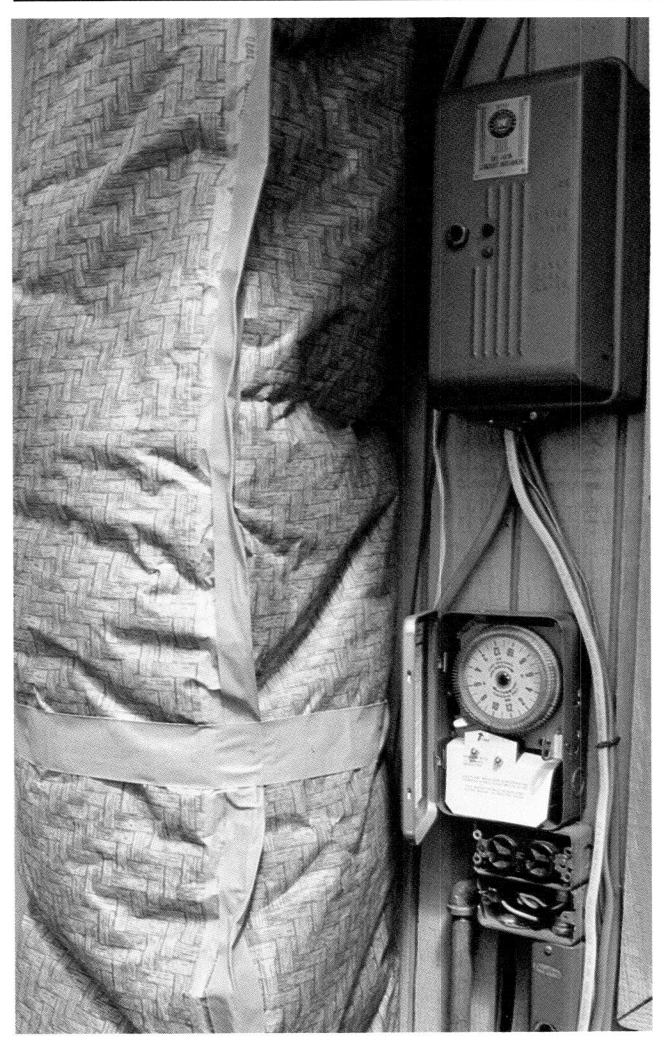

Professor Carnegie uses standard 8-inch air-conditioning duct to move the heated air from the collectors to rock storage.

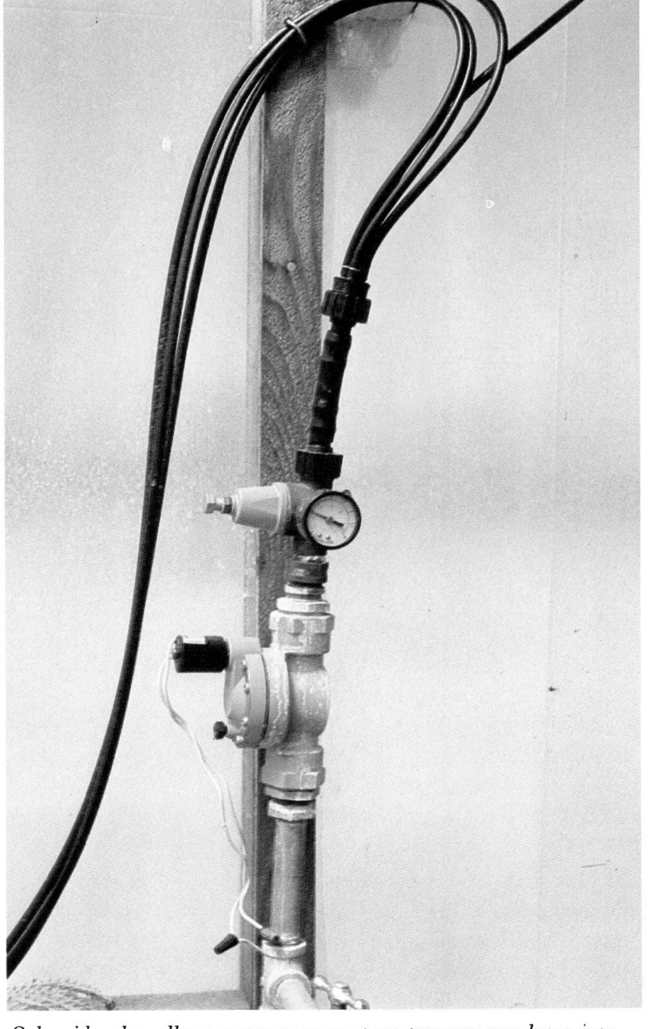

Solenoid valve allows water to move past pressure regulator into "spaghetti" tubing that delivers water to each plant individually.

Foundations and Floors

When thinking about insulation, too many people forget the floor and foundation. During the winter months in some areas, the ground is frozen many inches deep. That surface cold is a severe drain on greenhouse heat. To block it, put sheets of rigid insulation 1 or 2 inches thick around the outside of the foundation, from the footings to the top of the wall. An alternative is to dig a 4-inch wide trench down to the bottom of the footings and fill that with pumice stone.

The floor, particularly if brick, flagstone or concrete slab, is an effective heat sink. But its heat gain will be quickly lost if not insulated. Counter this by laying 4 inches of pumice rock beneath the flooring to insulate it. Water will still drain through.

If a cinder block wall is built for the north side of a lean-to greenhouse, the outside must be insulated to make sure heat radiating from the heat sink goes only into the greenhouse.

An Attached Solar Greenhouse

A solar greenhouse that is both beautiful and efficient has been built in Santa Fe, New Mexico. The owner, John Moseley, is a landscape architect as well as a talented builder and a student of solar techniques. This greenhouse is attached to the residence not merely for convenience but to utilize the excess greenhouse heat during the winter. In the summer, cooler air in the house is vented through the greenhouse to the outside.

The glass and redwood greenhouse is 8×14 feet and the roof is angled for maximum utilization of the summer sun. It is very similar in construction to the attached greenhouse described in Chapter 3. But in this case the top third of the roof is covered with insulation to provide relief from the overhead summer sun. Vents are installed as necessary.

The 14-foot north wall, the heat sink, is 8 feet high. It's made from pumice block poured full of concrete and the outside is insulated with 4-inch thick rigid insulation that was stuccoed to protect it from the weather. The low foundation for putting up the polyethylene wall in front—also insulated on the outside below ground level—is topped with bricks to follow the line of bricks on the territorial-style main house.

The front wall and the roof were originally designed to have only one pane of glass in each opening but a local code required two. The code also said

The solar greenhouse/residence of Santa Fe, New Mexico, landscape architect, John Moseley. The north wall of pumice block and concrete is the heat collector.

the glass windows must be separated at the corners, so the block wall was extended and a work area formed beside the outside entrance.

Construction started by laying out the area and setting up batter boards as detailed in Chapter 2. The ground was then excavated so the brick floor of the greenhouse, when finished, would be level with the floor of the residence. The two were connected by a sliding glass door after the greenhouse was finished.

With the excavation completed, slip forms of 1×4s for the footings were put around the inside perimeter and leveled all the way. The outside of the footings was formed with rigid insulation braced against the excavated wall.

When the footings had hardened, the walls were built with standard-size pumice blocks and insulation brought up to the ground level in front and on the sides. The front and side walls were poured full of pumice rock as an insulator. The back wall, the heat sink, was given maximum insulation on the outside.

In the frame, each vertical stud, plus the top and bottom plates and the crosspieces, were rabbetted to receive the panes of glass. If you don't have access to a table saw for rabbetting, the glass can be put in with quarter-round molding or 1×1 redwood strips as stops nailed to the studs and rafters.

The west wall, with the exterior door, was framed piece by piece, with the 2×6 door frame going in first, then the top plate, the door header, and the window and vent frames.

With the front and side walls in place, the next step was the roof. This was done a little differently than the conventional fashion of individually placing each rafter. The roof was measured and laid out just as if building a wall. The front end of the rafters were first cut so they would be in vertical line with the front wall. Like the front wall, each piece was rabbeted to accept the panes of glass, then the entire roof section was nailed together. Once it was lifted into place and toenailed to the top plate of the front wall, a 1×6 was used to cover this seam. At the back, where the roof extended above and slightly over the wall, the area was covered with plywood and insulated inside and outside.

The glass went in quickly, each piece sealed inside and outside with butyl rubber. The glass was held in place with strips of 1×2.

For the flooring, sand dug from a nearby dry stream bed was laid 3 inches thick over the ground. The sand was then dampened and leveled. Each brick was laid, tamped, and leveled as described earlier.

With the floor down, it was then a matter of finishing the benches and sink area before bringing in the plants and seedlings. By February, a month after it was completed, the greenhouse was filled with flowering plants and vegetables.

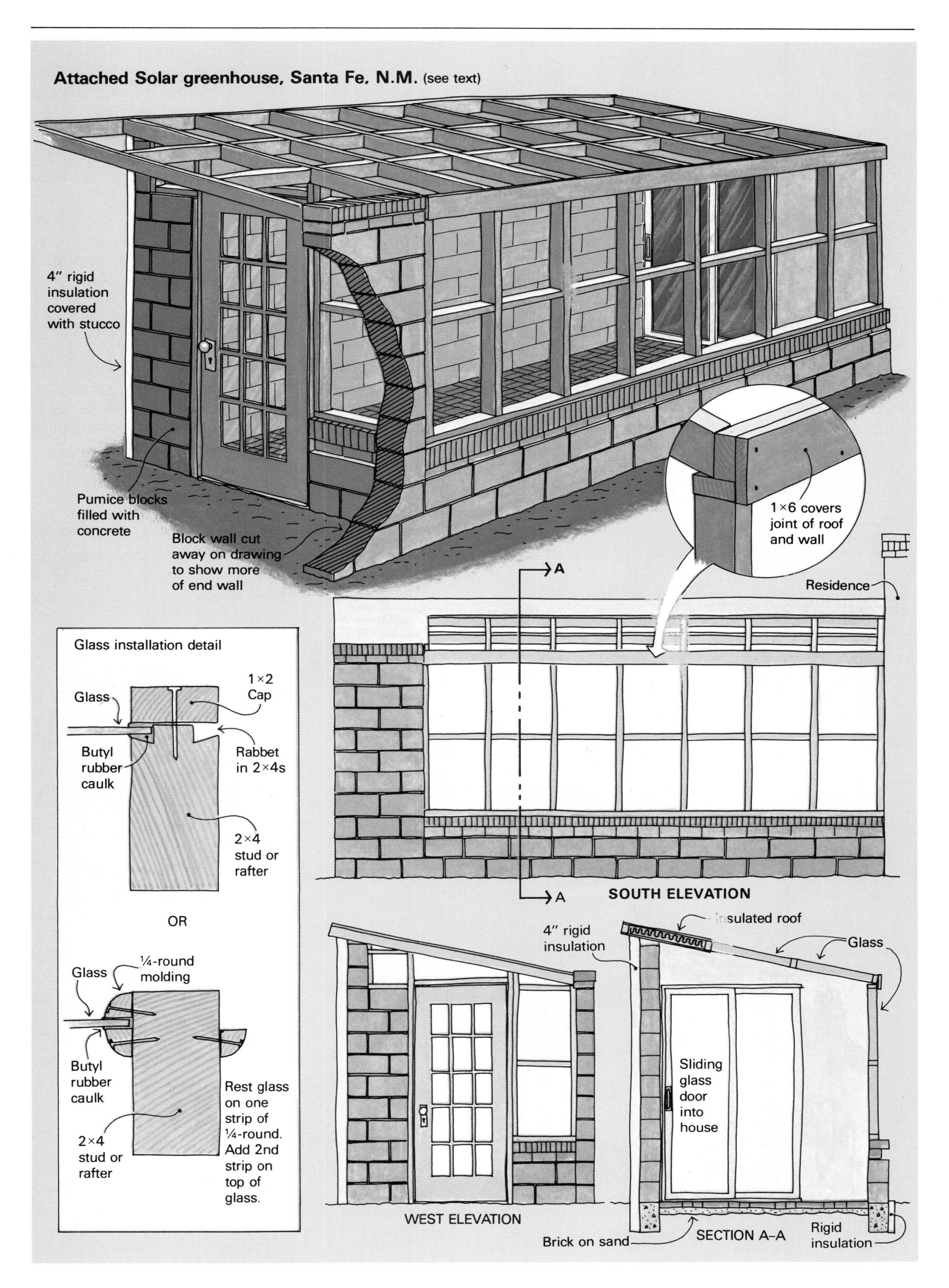
Attached Solar greenhouse, Santa Fe, N.M. (see text)
4" rigid insulation covered with stucco
Pumice blocks filled with concrete
Block wall cut away on drawing to show more of end wall
1×6 covers joint of roof and wall
Residence
A
A
SOUTH ELEVATION
Glass installation detail
Glass
1×2 Cap
Butyl rubber caulk
Rabbet in 2×4s
2×4 stud or rafter
OR
Glass
¼-round molding
Butyl rubber caulk
2×4 stud or rafter
Rest glass on one strip of ¼-round. Add 2nd strip on top of glass.
WEST ELEVATION
4" rigid insulation
Insulated roof
Glass
Sliding glass door into house
Brick on sand
SECTION A–A
Rigid insulation

An Angled-Wall Solar Greenhouse
First designed by New Mexico builder, Bill Yanda, this type of greenhouse is useful in areas with cold but fairly sunny winters and hot summers. The south wall is angled to directly face the low winter sun. But again, the top one-third of the roof is covered and insulated to give some respite inside from the summer sun. The angle of the front wall is generally 60°. To calculate the optimum angle for your own location, follow this rule of thumb: put the wall at an angle equal the geographical latitude plus 35°.

The amount of roof covering is important. In calculating this, you want the winter sun to strike high on the back wall which will be absorbing and storing heat. In the summer, about one-third of the greenhouse will be shaded but there can still be enough reflected light for good growing. Plants that love heat and sun should be moved to the front of the greenhouse in summer.

Once your foundation is down and the sill in place, the next step is to build the front walls. In this model, the south wall and roof have studs and rafters at intervals of 2 feet on center.

Before laying out the wall, cut the studs at the angle you wish. For a 60° slope, use a protractor to make a 30° angle on the bottom of the stud. The angle of the cut is always the difference between the vertical of 90° and the angle you want the wall to be. Cut the top of the stud parallel to the bottom so the top plate will lie flat. When all cut, lay the wall out, nail it together and put it in place with bracing at both ends.

The next step is to put up the rafters. If you can bolt one end to the overhang on your house, fine. Otherwise, put up a ledger board on the house and support each rafter with a joist hanger. You can cut expenses a little here by notching each rafter 1¼ inches and fitting them over the ledger board and then nailing into place.

For the front of the rafter to lie flat on the wall plate, you must cut what is called a "bird's mouth." To find this angle, hold one rafter in place at the outside end of the wall and mark where it needs to be cut. Use this rafter as a pattern board. When all are cut, toenail into place directly over each wall stud.

Now measure off the top third, more or less—depending on geographical latitude—of the roof rafters and mark, using a chalk line to snap all rafters at once. Nail 2×4 bracings straight across on this line, for this is where you will join the clear and solid portions of the roof.

Before going any further, put the end walls in place. The top plate on the end walls ties directly into the front wall plate. From this junction, run a stud down to the bottom plate. On the end where the door will be, use two studs nailed together on the side of the opening where you want to hang the door. Once the door is hung, measure off the door opening, allowing ¼ inch additional space for clearance, and put in the other side of the door frame. This stud should be cross-braced midway up the wall to either the adjoining stud or to the endwall stud that is tied to the side of the house.

On the front wall between each rafter, nail in a 2×4 so it is flush with the top of the rafters. You may have to use a ripsaw here for an even, tight fit. The next step is to cover all crosspieces on the roof with strips of corrugated molding—foam, redwood or rubber. You are almost ready to put up the corrugated panels on the roof.

First, drill out the nail holes in each panel. Along the top edge, which will be covered by the solid portion of the roof, put holes on top of every third ridge. Along the bottom, which will be pulled at by winds, put an aluminum nail with neoprene washer on every ridge.

Now, across the upper edge of the fiberglass roof, lay in another strip of molding, right on top of the fiberglass, and add a bead of sealant. Then put the solid panels of ⅜-inch exterior grade plywood in place. Allow it to overlap the fiberglass by 4 inches, to keep rain from blowing in. You can use corrugated steel as the opaque part of the roof, which will mesh evenly with the corrugated fiberglass, but it is difficult to vent.

If the back of the roof is not under an overhang, metal flashing must be used between it and the house. At any rate, this area must be tightly sealed. The plywood can then be covered with composition or cedar shingles, or painted.

On the front and side walls, use flat fiberglass panels. Before nailing in each panel, put down a bead of sealant and make sure the panel is square. Nail every 6 inches with flathead galvanized 4d nails. When all pieces are up, lay another bead of sealant along the joints and cover with a strip of redwood lath.

To the solid roof inside, staple in fiberglass insulation and then cover with wood or paneling of your choice. This area, like the whole interior, should be painted white to reflect light back into the greenhouse.

Finally, to create the dead-air insulating barrier, cover the interior with 4 mil polyethylene film of the type resistant to ultraviolet light.

Walls are built on the ground, then raised when ready to connect together. Studs and rafters are spaced 2 feet apart, on center.

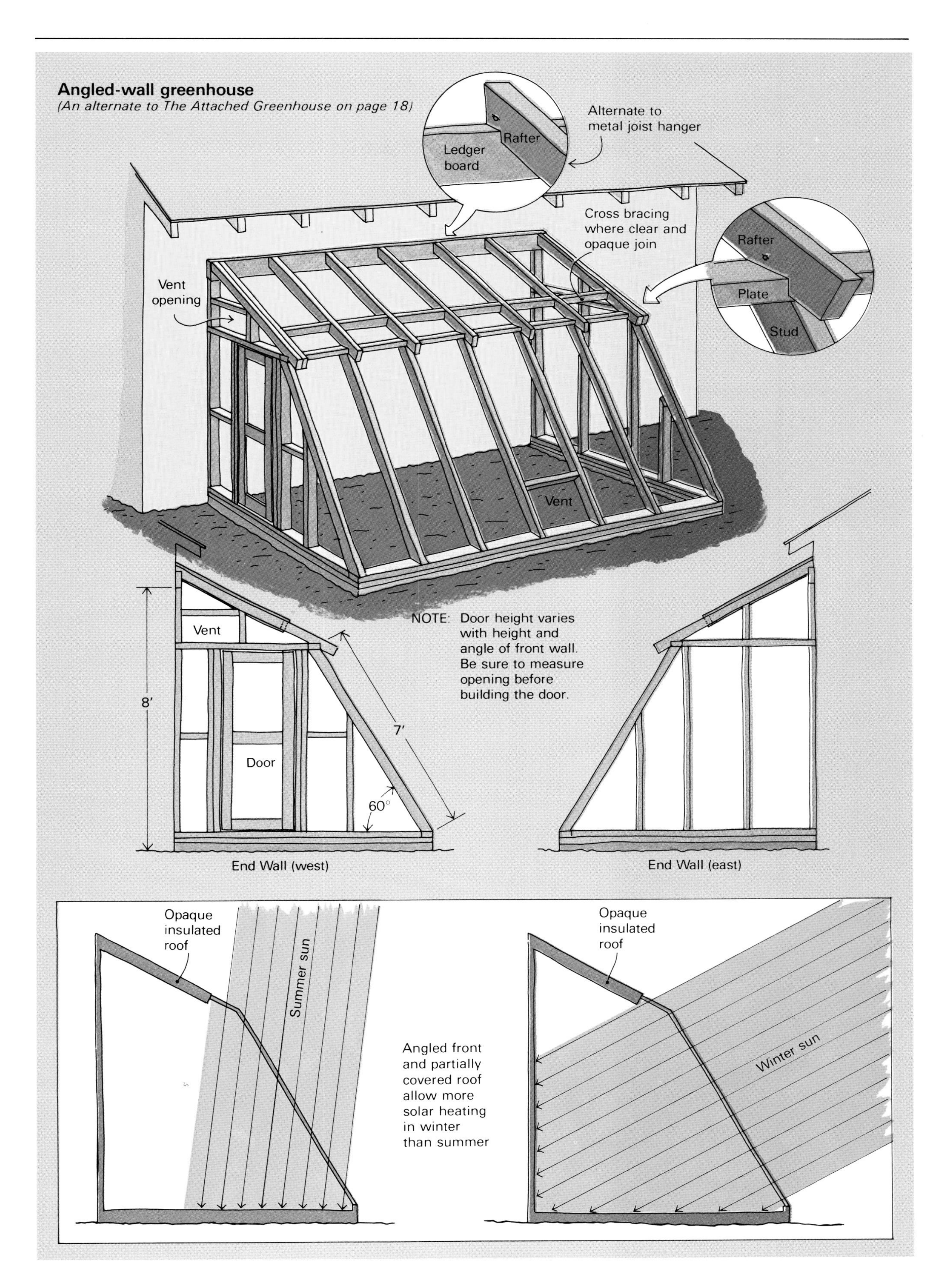
Angled-wall greenhouse
(An alternate to The Attached Greenhouse on page 18)
Ledger board
Rafter
Alternate to metal joist hanger
Cross bracing where clear and opaque join
Rafter
Plate
Stud
Vent opening
Vent
Vent
8′
7′
Door
60°
NOTE: Door height varies with height and angle of front wall. Be sure to measure opening before building the door.
End Wall (west)
End Wall (east)
Opaque insulated roof
Summer sun
Angled front and partially covered roof allow more solar heating in winter than summer
Opaque insulated roof
Winter sun

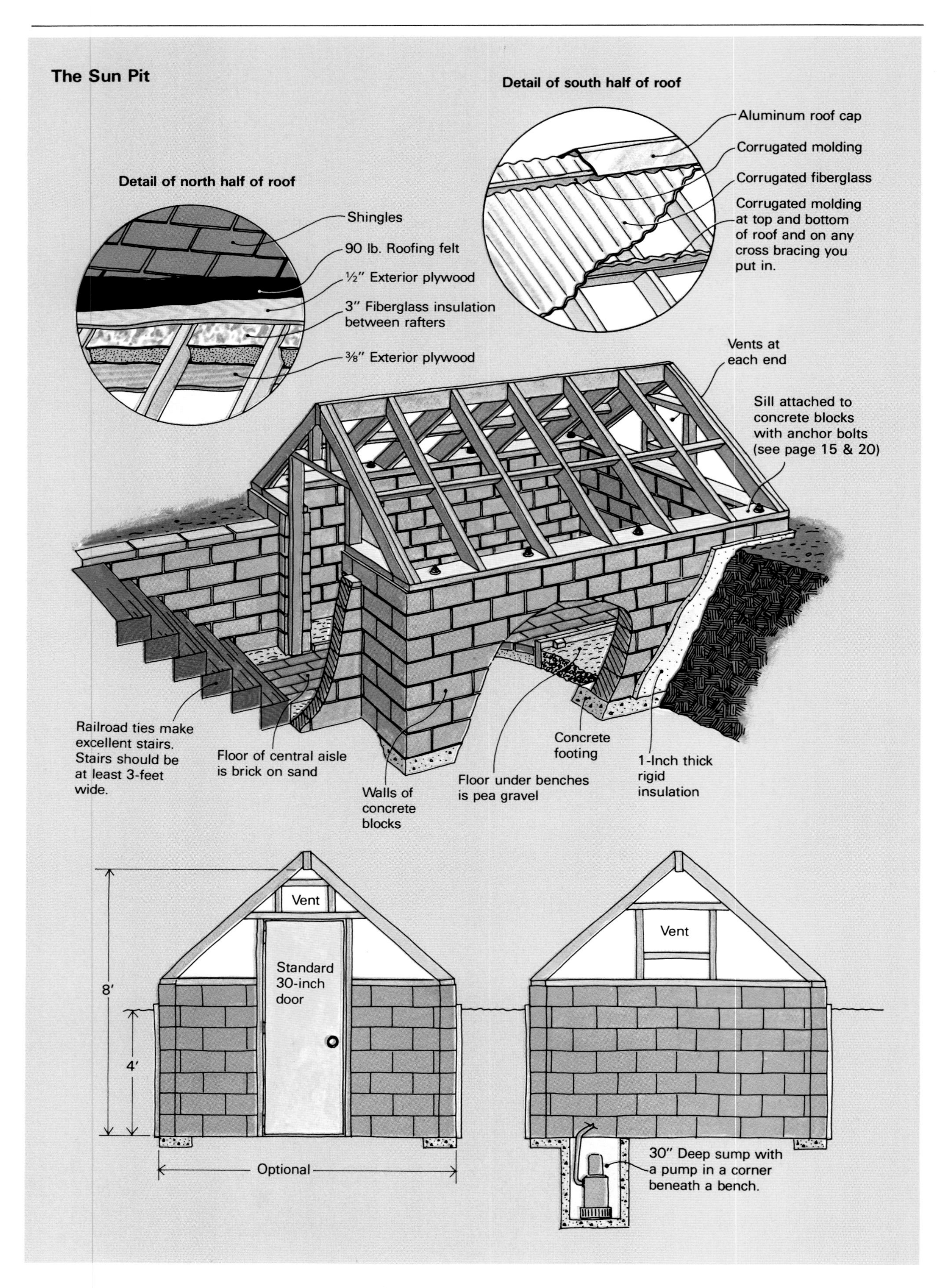

The Sun Pit
Detail of south half of roof
Aluminum roof cap
Corrugated molding
Corrugated fiberglass
Corrugated molding at top and bottom of roof and on any cross bracing you put in.
Detail of north half of roof
Shingles
90 lb. Roofing felt
½" Exterior plywood
3" Fiberglass insulation between rafters
⅜" Exterior plywood
Vents at each end
Sill attached to concrete blocks with anchor bolts (see page 15 & 20)
Railroad ties make excellent stairs. Stairs should be at least 3-feet wide.
Floor of central aisle is brick on sand
Walls of concrete blocks
Floor under benches is pea gravel
Concrete footing
1-Inch thick rigid insulation
Vent
Standard 30-inch door
8'
4'
Optional
Vent
30" Deep sump with a pump in a corner beneath a bench.

The Sun Pit

One thinks of growing things *in* the ground, not below it. But the sun pit, which puts you into the earth with a clear roof overhead, is a particularly efficient means to grow things year-round. Called by some a cold frame with head room, the sun pit requires little or no additional heating. It takes advantage of the natural insulation of the ground and has little heat loss through the walls to the soil. Its low profile protects it from the wind. If you put it close to your house, you can use the extra heat from the pit to warm your house.

Like most greenhouses, a sun pit soon proves to be too small. So in building it give yourself plenty of room. A bare minimum size is 8×12 feet but 12×18 feet would allow you to have growing space on both sides of the pit and down the middle.

First, mark out the area where you want the sun pit, locating it on the east-west axis with one length of the roof facing south. The next important thing to remember is not to get carried away and dig the pit by yourself. If you can't convince your spouse and offspring to help you, hire a backhoe. This powerful tractor with a scoop bucket on one end and a hydraulic digging arm on the other can normally be hired for under $30 an hour. A moderate-size backhoe should be able to dig the pit and remove the dirt in less than two hours.

The pit should be 4 feet deep. Once it is dug, square the sides until they are vertical and level the floor: use a level on top of a straight 2×4 to check it. Around the edge, dig a ditch 4 inches deep and 12 inches wide for the footings, which should be poured with the aid of leveling stakes as previously described, and a sump 30 inches deep and about 18 inches wide from which irrigation and seepage water can be pumped out of the pit. While waiting for the footings to dry, dig your steps at the end away from prevailing winter winds. Also, bring in your water and electricity lines at this time.

When the footings are cured, start laying up the cinder block wall. It must be insulated on the outside with a minimum of 1-inch thick rigid insulation or 4 inches of pumice rock.

When putting up the wall, instead of mortaring each block in place, lay a course of blocks and then fill every other opening with concrete and tamp thoroughly. Once that concrete has stiffened, lay up another course and fill the alternate holes. Keep checking the level and plumb of the wall as you go.

The next step is to finish the flooring while you can still get a wheelbarrow in. At this depth, the ground will be relatively warm and insulation under the floor is not necessary. You may cover the floor with 4 inches of pea gravel or the more attractive brick on sand. As a compromise, put the gravel under the benches, holding it in place with 2×6s, and cover the walkways with sand and brick.

Once the flooring, water and electricity have been installed, you're ready to start the roof. For the conventional A-frame style, start by erecting a 2×6 ridge board directly down the center of the pit. This should be about 8 feet above the floor but you may adjust to your own height and needs.

To find the angle of end cuts so the rafters will fit smoothly against the ridge board and the sills, hold one rafter in place at the end, mark it, and use it as a pattern for the other rafters. For a 12-foot long sun pit, cut 18 rafters. This gives you double rafters on each end to provide a good nailing surface for the end walls. The end walls should be spaced 2 feet on center with vent openings directly under the ridge.

For a sun pit without electrically-operated fans, install vent openings on the north slope of the roof near the peak. Space them every other rafter.

Cover the north slope of the roof with ½-inch plywood topped with 90-pound roofing felt and then with the covering of your choice, such as shingles. Inside, staple 3-inch fiberglass insulation between the studs and cover with 3-inch exterior grade plywood. This ceiling should be painted white to reflect light back onto the plants.

The south wall is covered with 4-foot wide sheets of Tedlar-treated corrugated fiberglass. The top and bottom of each panel should be fitted over corrugated foam molding and nailed on every other ridge. Cover the ridge of the roof with an aluminum roof cap, remembering to put down another layer of foam molding between it and the fiberglass for a tight seal.

The end walls can be covered with glass set between the stud openings or with flat fiberglass. In really cold areas, where snow is a problem, cover and insulate the end walls.

A word of caution: Sun pits are difficult to heat and ventilate, and controlling plant diseases can also be a problem. They were once popular as commercial greenhouses but fell out of favor about the turn of the century because of their inefficiencies. Still, with careful management, a sun pit can be an inexpensive and satisfactory type of home greenhouse.

Insulated by the earth, the sun pit is among the basic types of solar greenhouses.

Hydroponics

The basics of hydroponics, from high maintenance to automated systems. How to build and use your own system, with details on aggregates, solutions, sanitation, pumps, sumps and nutrient flow techniques.

For many people, hydroponics conjures up images of alchemy, of convoluted systems of tanks, pipes and strange bubbling solutions that make plants mysteriously grow without soil. Even worse are complex formulas that trigger bad memories of high school chemistry.

In fact, growing plants by hydroponics is an exciting way to produce vegetables for your table and flowers for the house. And a hydroponic unit works equally well if you put it on the patio for the summer or in the greenhouse for year-round production.

Hydroponics is becoming so easy that more and more people are turning to it. There are commercial setups on the market but you can make your own because the system is not complex. And the nutrient mixes are now readily available in nurseries or garden supply stores, so never mind if you barely passed chemistry.

Hydroponics is simply growing plants in a solution of nutrients rather than in soil. In the garden, plants are anchored in the soil and draw water and nutrients from it. In hydroponics, a water solution rich with the necessary foods is washed or pumped through a mix of light gravel that both anchors the plants and retains the solution. There is nothing mystical about this process, which also goes under such names as aquaculture, soilless gardening and nutriculture.

'Tropic' tomatoes grown in greenhouse hydroponically.

Advantages

In today's world, space is increasingly at a premium. The availability of individual houses with a yard out front and a garden in back is barely keeping up with the demand. Yet people still want to grow plants and vegetables. Hydroponics is a solution, so to speak.

Plants and crops can be grown almost anywhere hydroponically, from a greenhouse to a small apartment. The system works best, however, in a greenhouse with ample light and humidity.

Tomatoes, squash, and sweetpeas in hydroponic container on patio.

There is less work with hydroponics than a conventional garden. Certainly you aren't out there every day tilling the soil, pulling weeds or yelling at the neighbor's dog for running through your lettuce. Usually, about 20 minutes a day will keep your nutriculture garden flourishing. With automation, even less time is needed.

Advocates of hydroponics proclaim their yields are bigger, which may be true, and even say the vegetables taste better. Weather damage is nonexistent. Disease is minimized if proper protections are carried out.

Finally, in times when the country seems to be running short of everything, including the clean water that we always took for granted, there is great conservation practiced in hydroponics. The same nutrient solution in most systems is used repeatedly for one to four weeks. The old solution is not thrown away but is poured around trees or plants outside to give them a lift.

Disadvantages

Hydroponics, unfortunately, does not mean the elimination of all work. Plants grown this way respond even more rapidly to poor growing conditions than they do to good ones. To insure against loss, plants must be inspected closely and frequently.

Setting up the system takes time. Boxes to hold the aggregate mix must be built or bought, pipes installed and pumps hooked up.

Background

History indicates that plants and vegetables have been grown in different water cultures for hundreds of years. The first big advance came nearly three centuries ago with John Woodward, an English chemist and Fellow of the Royal Society. In 1699, Woodward began using mint plants in an attempt to learn if plants received their food through the soil or water. Using rain water, tap water and river water from the Thames, he found that the more soil added, the better the plant grew.

His experiments did not extend much beyond that, and it wasn't until 1804 that Nicolas de Saussure proved that plants need a combination of air, soil and water. Shortly thereafter, French scientist Jean Boussingault raised crops in beds of sand and charcoal that were periodically flooded with nutrient solutions.

Not until 1929, however, did hydroponics as we know it today begin. The word hydroponics is credited to William F. Gericke, a professor at the University of California at Berkeley, who set up a successful hydroponic system where plants grew without any soil whatsoever. As word of tomato plants reaching 20 feet in height, plus other spectacular results with flowers and vegetables, began to spread, commercial hydroponics started to take off. It still is expanding, and is widely used in many parts of the world for its speed and efficiency in vegetable production.

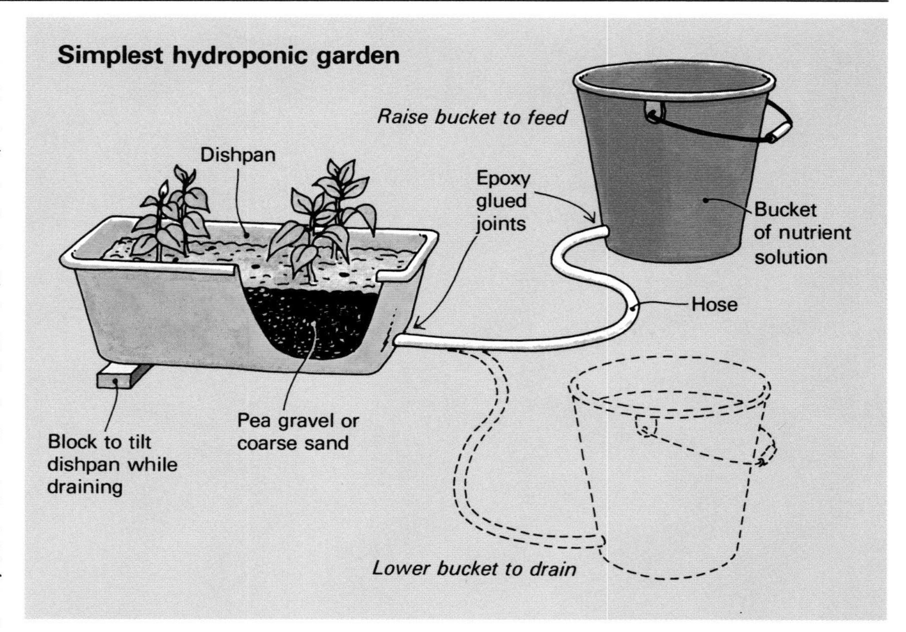

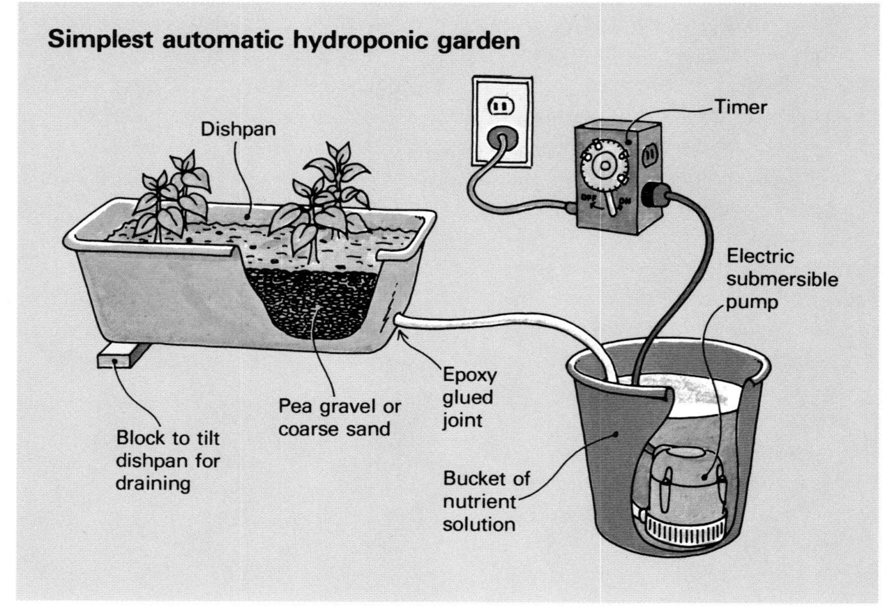

Basic System

A simple hydroponic system that you can make from items you probably have around the kitchen can be set up in an hour. It's simple but it has all the elements of a more sophisticated system and it works fine.

You need nothing more than a dishpan, some clean gravel or coarse sand, a length of plastic or rubber hose and bucket.

Cut a hole in the side of both the dishpan and the bucket right near the bottom for the hose. It should fit tightly and be sealed with an epoxy glue. Fill the dishpan with 6 to 8 inches of pea gravel. Move yourself and the system to a sunny protected spot and pour the nutrient solution into the bucket.

Plant four to six pepper plants in the dishpan, then raise the bucket until the growing bed in the pan is submerged by the solution. Next, lower the bucket and let the solution from the tilted dishpan drain back into the bucket. Do this once in the morning and once at night. Simple as that. And you will have more peppers than you can eat.

Automated System

While the above system with a bucket works well, it requires your attention twice a day. To escape that obligation and to make sure you don't forget to run the solution through, use a more advanced system with a small electric pump and timer. The principle, however, remains the same: saturate the growing medium, then let it drain. The root hairs will find the needed moisture and nutrients on the damp gravel and will still receive air.

This larger automated system requires a growing bed and a nearby sump. A large plastic garbage can or bucket works fine for the sump. An electric pump that is plugged into a timer runs the nutrient solution into the growing tray at the prescribed hour in the morning. The solution drains from the tray back into the sump. That afternoon the process is repeated.

Aggregates
Although flowers and vegetables have been grown with no soil at all—roots just suspended in a mist of nutrient solution—the easiest and most practical way is to use some kind of a "soil." The plants are thus able to anchor themselves and grow as if they were out in the garden. They won't know they're not in the garden if you don't tell them.

The most common form of aggregate is pea gravel, the medium-coarse grade of about ¼ to ⅜ inch in size. Any larger than that and the solution tends to drain too rapidly and the roots will dry out too quickly. The aggregate should be free of calcium or limestone. Ordinary sand can be used but by itself it is heavy and slow to drain. The risk of fungi and even drowning the roots increases.

Mixtures of sand and light gravel or sand and a little vermiculite are acceptable. Vermiculite alone generally retains too much water. Sawdust has been used but absorbs too much solution and does not drain properly.

For the beginner, stick with the proven success of a light gravel. Not only does it fill and drain at the right speed but it is easily sterilized

Hydroponic system designed by Pacific Aquaculture, Sausalito, California. Lower box is nutrient solution reservoir. Submersible pump fills top box at timed intervals. Rooting medium is Pumalite.

Solutions
One of the advantages of hydroponics is that you know your plants are receiving all the nutrients they need, provided you have the right mix.

There are numerous formulas for solutions available but unless you are inclined to chemical experiment or plan a large scale operation, the premixed commercial formulas are recommended.

Whether you mix your own or buy a commercial solution, you will have to check its pH level after it is poured over the aggregate. The pH tells you if the solution is acid or alkaline. Most garden supply stores have various kits for measuring this. The pH scale runs from 1 to 14, with 7 being neutral. The ideal growing level is slightly acid, or 6.5 on the pH scale.

Your growing solution should be checked every three days while running through the aggregate. In most cases you will not have to make adjustments but if it is above 7, it is too alkaline. To reduce the alkaline and increase the acid, use an eye dropper to add sulphuric acid—don't spill any on yourself—to the solution in the holding tank. Add a few drops and recheck. The next time you run it through the aggregate, check again until it is adjusted. If it becomes too acid, add sodium hydroxide to push the pH up.

Another trick you can try is adding white vinegar to increase acidity and some baking soda to increase alkalinity.

pH test kits

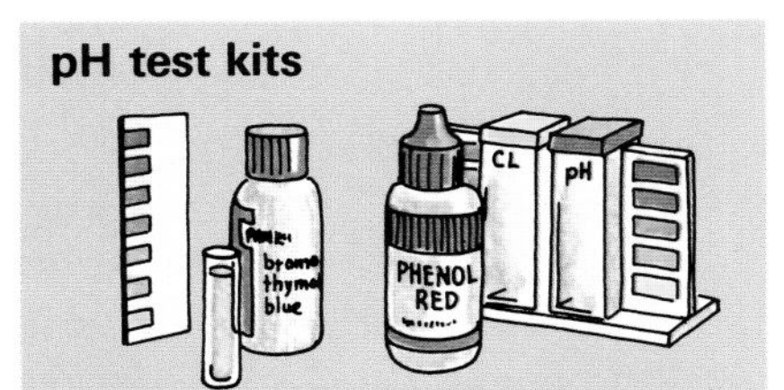

Kits for testing the pH of swimming pool or fish aquarium water work on hydroponic nutrient solutions, too.

Sanitation
It is essential for the hydroponic gardener in a greenhouse to take several precautions against diseases. Some root fungi can spread with alarming rapidity because the solution moves from roots to roots. This is not always the case, however.

The more serious gardeners change shoes before entering the greenhouse and slip on clean coveralls to minimize the risk of infecting their plants.

One not uncommon disease is the tobacco mosaic virus. Once established, it is hard to eradicate. To prevent this, don't allow smoking—or chewing—in your hydroponic greenhouse.

Different Growing Beds
There are a wide variety of containers to hold the growing bed and nutrients. These range from the simple dishpan and bucket already mentioned to wooden or fiberglass frames. But the essentials are the same: it must be leakproof and it must rapidly fill and drain.

Some people cut 55-gallon drums in half lengthwise and coat the interiors with fiberglass to make growing beds. Others simply build a 2×4 frame on the floor of the greenhouse, line it with a plastic vinyl and fill it with gravel. There are also commercially made fiberglass growing beds available. Find what suits you best, but here's a basic setup. Adjust these measurements for your own needs.

Start by making a box 8 feet long and 2 feet wide from 1×8s. Make the bottom from a sheet of exterior grade plywood. Put a 1×2 across the top center to prevent the sides from bowing out. Glue all the joints with epoxy glue and caulk the seams. Then paint the interior with three coats of fiberglass for the best results. Or you can

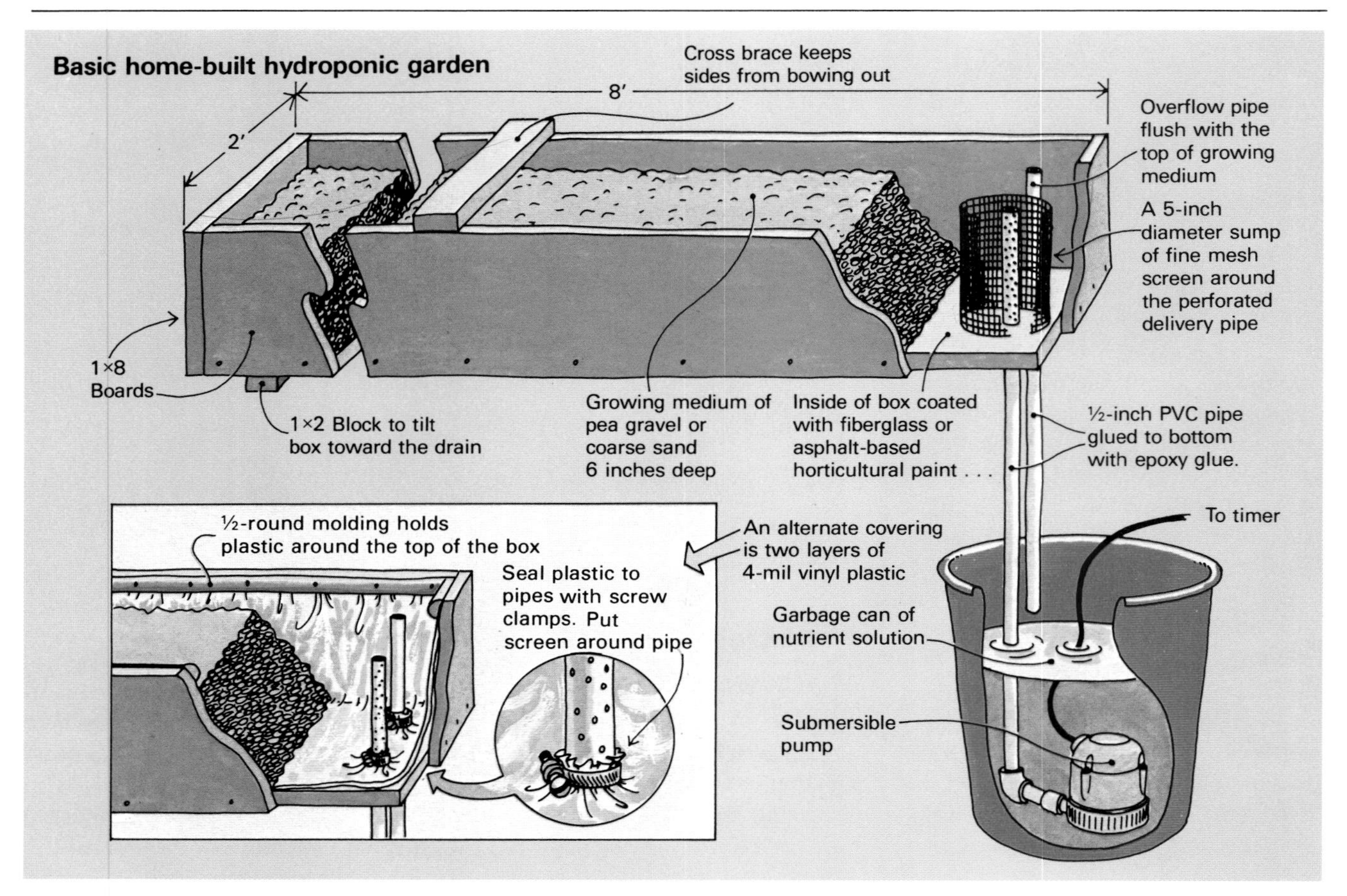

use a horticultural asphalt-base paint.

A common alternative to protecting wood with some kind of paint is to line the box with two layers of 4 mil plastic vinyl. Two layers are used in case one has a pinhole leak in it. Anywhere a pipe enters the box, gather a little of the plastic around the pipe and use a screw-type hose clamp to make it tight and leak resistant. The plastic can be held around the top of the box with a piece of half-round molding.

Raise the opposite end of the bed about ¾ inch by nailing a strip of 1×2 across the bottom. With the box up on a bench, this allows the solution pumped into the bed to drain back to the sump by gravity flow.

The nutrient solution can be delivered to the bed in several different ways. One is to have the PVC pipe part of both the pump and drain systems. This can be accomplished with a pipe running the length of the growing bed beneath the medium with ¼-inch holes in it every few inches. Or, as shown in the drawing, a perforated pipe about 6 inches long protected from the growing medium by a sump of wire mesh. The wire mesh allows you to clean the holes in the pipe periodically without digging up the medium. The solution is thus delivered to the bed and then drained back through the pump.

Other delivery systems route the pipe over the top of the bed and use small spaghetti tubing to deliver the solution to all parts of the bed.

It is advisable to add an overflow pipe at the lower end. Run the pipe through a hole next to the drain and make the top of it flush with the top of the growing medium. It should either tie into the drain pipe or run directly back to the sump.

Of Pumps and Sumps

With the box completed, the next step is to supply it with the nutrient solution so you can start planting. Since the growing box is generally on a bench to allow you to garden with ease, the other apparatus can go under the bench. This consists of a small plastic garbage can or bucket to hold the solution and a small electric pump. The amount of solution will vary with the type of growing medium used. Experiment to find how much you need.

The pump is submersible and sits at the bottom of the solution container. Hook it to the PVC pipe in the growing box with a length of plastic hose or with more PVC pipe. PVC is readily available, cuts with an ordinary saw and the joints glue together in seconds.

Now, connect the pump to a timer that plugs into a nearby socket set to flood the box once in the morning and once in the evening.

The box will fill to the top and then should drain in 10 or 15 minutes. Faster draining is all right, but the roots must not be submerged for more than 30 minutes or they will drown.

A system in which the solution is fed to the roots from below is termed "sub-irrigation." There are other systems, including misting and pumping water on top of the aggregate, but they are more complex. This method is a proven success.

Once the growing bed, the pump and sump are set up, you can run several boxes at once. Put the boxes in a line and connect the tubes in front with T-fittings. The pump will fill all the boxes at once with this manifold hook up.

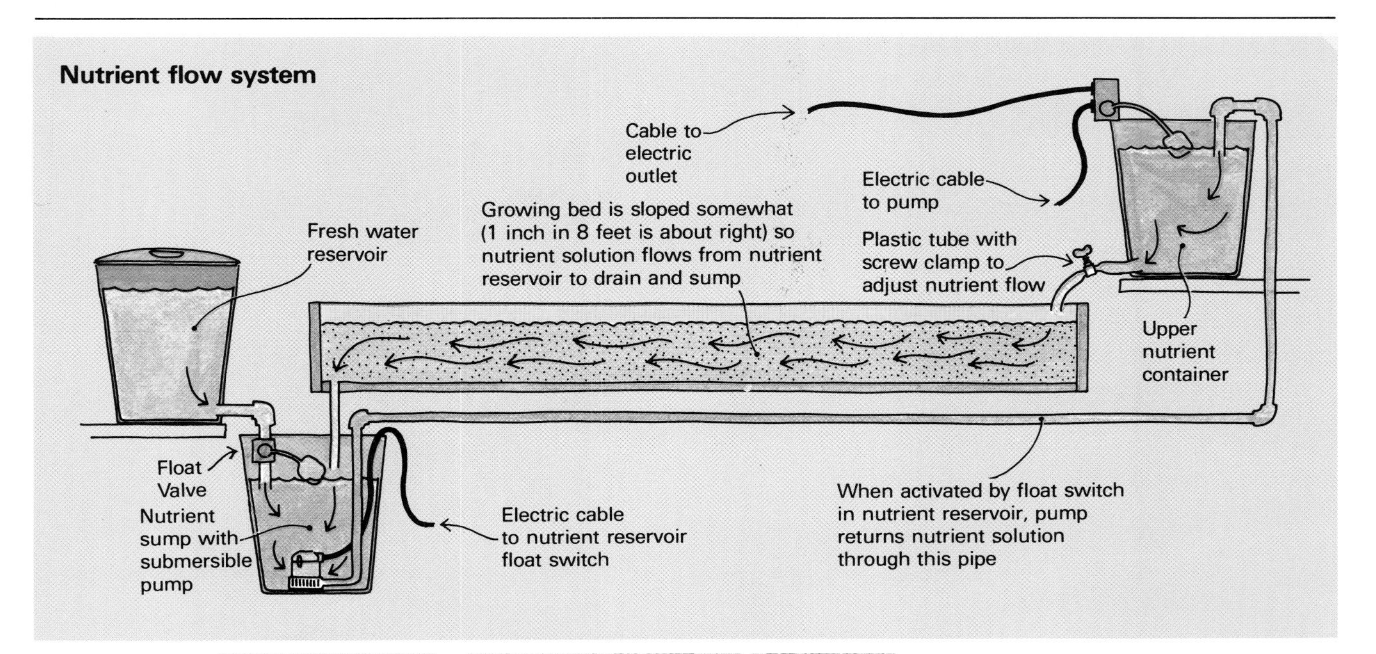

Mrs. Whyte, Strawberry Point, California, uses her hydroponic greenhouse for much of her family's fresh food. Squash blossoms have become a diet favorite as well as more familiar corn, broccoli, cucumbers, beets, and chard.

Nutrient Flow Techniques

One of the new developments in hydroponic gardening is called the nutrient flow technique (NFT). It was first developed by British scientist Dr. A. J. Cooper and then further modified by Dr. Paul A. Schippers at Cornell University. This new approach calls for a continuous flow of nutrients, slow but steady, rather than the more commonly used method of periodic flooding. The NFT is disarmingly simple and, barring a power failure, able to run by itself for days at a time.

The system incorporates the sump, pump and growing beds previously described. The big difference is a nutrient solution container mounted at one end and slightly above the growing bed. The solution is released from the high container into the growing bed through a small rubber hose. A screw clamp on the hose adjusts the amount of nutrient flow.

The growing bed is angled at a slope of 1:100 or more to keep the nutrients flowing through the growing medium.

The solution runs from the growing bed into the sump where a submersible pump runs the solution back into the upper holding basin.

The pump is controlled by a float switch mounted in the upper basin. When the solution drops enough, the pump is activated until the float rises enough to shut off the pump.

A float valve in the lower holding

tank admits fresh water from a water barrel when the solution level drops too low because of transpiration and evaporation.

Dr. Schippers has also devised a simple channel-bed system for growing smaller plants such as lettuce, spinach or Chinese cabbage. To make the bed, nail 2×4s about 6 inches apart to a 4×8-foot sheet of plywood and then cover it with black polyethylene to form the troughs. At the top, the nutrient solution is put in each channel through a manifold system. It is drained from the other end back to the sump.

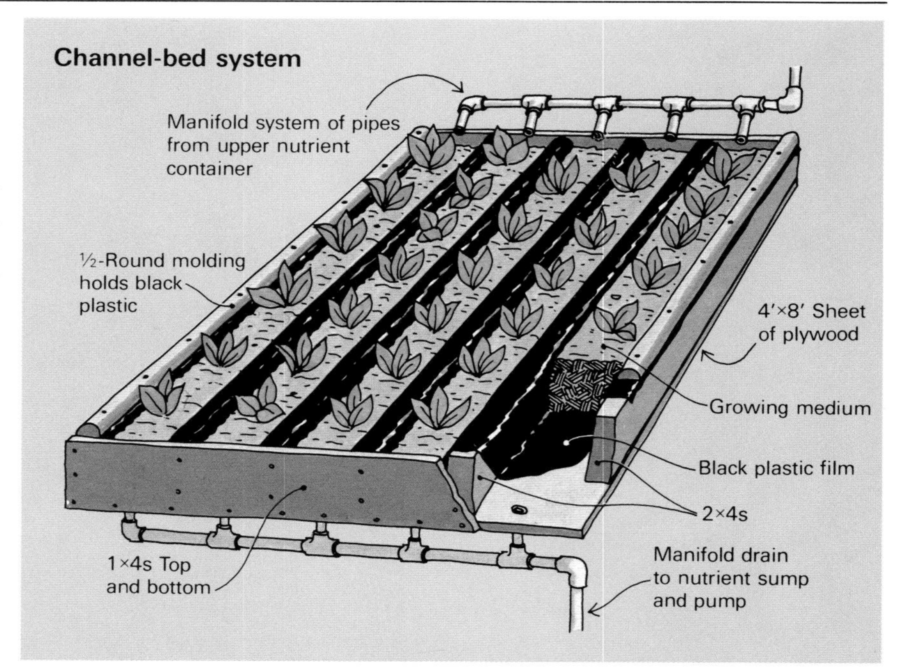

Make it Grow Right

With everything set up, it's time to plant. Larger seeds that will not wash away can be sprouted directly in the growing box. Set them in the aggregate by making a small hole with your finger or using a short length of PVC pipe to place them. Tiny seeds can be set in small paper cups with the bottoms removed and filled with a mixture of gravel and vermiculite to hold more moisture. Set these directly in the growing bed.

Seedlings can be transplanted directly to the growing mix but even if the roots are washed, the risk of also transplanting a fungus is increased. Seedlings can also be germinated between two damp paper towels and then transplanted.

Detail of Pacific Aquaculture system. Water or nutrient solution is added to reservoir through end slot. Nutrients added twice per month; changed once per month; pH checked every week. Time clock controls pump. Plants are tomatoes and beans.

The planting bed should normally be filled and drained twice a day. But during the summer months, when it's hot and dry, you may have to increase this to three or even four times a day. It will not hurt the plants to be flooded more often as long as there is proper drainage, but letting the roots dry out may do irreparable damage. This is why the nutrient flow technique promises better growing conditions.

The growing medium should remain damp, like a wrung out wash cloth, at all times. Once the operation is underway you and your hydroponic garden will adjust to each other and you will almost instinctively know if the plants are doing their best.

During the hot months, the water in the solution will evaporate more rapidly. Check periodically to see that the solution level is kept at 90 percent or more of the original level. Otherwise the nutrient salts may become too concentrated and burn the roots.

You will also learn quickly how the plants are doing on the nutrient mix you give them. For best results, start by changing this solution every week. But gradually extend the changing time, all the while watching to see if your plants show any sign of wilt. Gardeners commonly go two, even four, weeks on each batch but there are many variables, so experiment and watch the plants carefully.

Finally, be sure to flood the growing container with fresh water every two weeks. This washes away the buildup of residual nutrient salts that could eventually damage the roots. Don't forget this important little task.

Sterilizing the Bed

Even if diseases never invade your hydroponic garden, it is a good idea to sterilize the bed at least once a year. However, if your plants are attacked and killed, you will have to remove them and sterilize the bed completely. Here are two good ways.

The first is to use a mixture of chlorine and water. This is the same thing that keeps swimming pools clean but your mixture is considerably stronger. Mix 1½ ounces of liquid chlorine in 10 gallons of water. Plug the end drain hole and fill the box until the growing aggregate is fully submerged. Let it soak 24 hours, then drain and throw away the chlorine solution. Flood and drain the box with fresh water three times a day for the next two days, and then you're ready to plant again.

Above, hydroponic garden of Swiss chard, sweet peas, marigolds, and cherry tomatoes. Control box times submersible pump and greenhouse temperature. Electric outlets are for accessories such as plant grow lights. Left, StemGem clips hold tomato stems to string. Strings dangle loose and plants sway in breeze.

Final Reminders

The plants in a hydroponic garden cannot survive on the nutrients alone. They must be in balance with the complete growing cycle. This includes:

1. Ample Light: The plants must have light for photosynthesis to take place. If they can receive only a little sunlight, then supplement it with fluorescent lighting, or even grow them entirely under fluorescent lights.
2. Correct Temperature: A plant's response to heat regulates its rate of growth. Most plants do well in the range of 65° to 75° F (18° to 24° C) while others require a more extreme temperature.
3. Balanced Nutrients: By checking the pH level and watching how plants respond the longer you let the solution remain, you will keep your operation a success. But the pH balance must be maintained.

You can probably grow almost any plant you like in your hydroponic tank but some grow more easily than others: in fact, so luxuriously that you may find you've planted too closely. When you start your first crop of any plant, give the individuals lots of room. Interplanting is great for some of the slower-growing crops. For instance, spacing your tomatoes on 18-inch centers will encourage top production. Interplant with fast-maturing crops like lettuce and radishes.

Be careful to follow the manufacturer's directions in changing the growing medium. Salt and toxicity problems can develop if you don't circulate the medium properly or change it soon enough. Most disease problems are avoided entirely by following directions carefully. Don't use too much or too little of the mineral mixture: the plants need the proper balance.

Experiment with different varieties of a particular crop until you find the one that does best in your unit. You may want to try new crops every year —peaches, grapes or strawberries. You can also use different methods of support for your plants—strings, stakes and trellises. You can have great fun with your hydroponic unit if you grow unusual things out of season for the delight of your friends, your family and yourself.

Coldframes, Hotbeds & Laths

Construction and use details on a variety of coldframes, hotbeds, raised bed covers, hotcaps and shady retreats.

Some gardeners are especially determined. They're determined to harvest a crop despite the odds of weather, season length, or handicaps such as excessive shade. They may not always succeed in harvesting that late crop of tomatoes or corn, but ideas of the determined gardener are always interesting, if not unique.

The creed of the determined gardener is to find a way to "cheat the season," either by lengthening it, making it warmer or cooler, wetter or drier, adding or reducing sunlight, or by providing protection from the wind.

This chapter is written about and for these gardeners. Here we will talk about the old and the new from our own test garden and the gardens of others. We will explore coldframes, hotbeds, row covers, and row caps plus an array of unique home-made season cheaters, in the pages that follow.

Coldframes

Talking about coldframes first is actually starting in the middle. Coldframes begin to approach the greenhouse in capability, and compared with some of the other concepts which we'll be dealing with later, they are much larger and more substantial structures.

Coldframe is, in fact, a term applied to many types of structures. Around the turn of this century, no farm garden was complete without one. Their biggest disadvantage is that they don't have the room to accommodate both the gardener and his or her plants.

Structurally, a coldframe is a bottomless, usually glass-covered box, heated only by the sun. It should be air tight, treated with a wood preservative, and sunk into the ground. Its hinged transparent window can be stock cold frame "sash" (available from greenhouse supply firms), an old window or glass door, fiberglass, or polyethylene-film.

Orient the coldframe to the south in order to receive maximum winter sunlight. (See illustration, page 7.) A fence or wall on the north side provides wind protection. White or silver paint on the inside walls helps reflect more light to the plants. If you want to adapt an old door frame or window, notch the horizontal mullions or pane dividers to facilitate water runoff.

Place a thermometer inside the frame and shield it from the direct rays of the sun. Watch it for a few weeks and you'll learn how the temperature fluctuates. When the temperature is high, open the sash to permit air circulation. Close it again when temperatures start to drop to conserve radiation absorbed by the soil.

In actual practice, the frames are usually opened in the morning and then closed as soon as the sun's direct rays have passed over. Another possibility is to equip the frame with a small, thermostatically controlled fan.

During hot weather, consider cooling the coldframe with shadecloth, a lath, a mist sprayer, or other methods similar to those used in a greenhouse.

One of our test garden coldframes has exchangeable panels. During coolest weather, the fiberglass (top) retains heat. Lath (center) allows maximum air exchange. Shade cloth (bottom) reduces light and wind for the most tender seedlings.

Opposite page, tomato seeds germinate quickly under this miniature, fiberglass row cover.

Uses of the Coldframe

Here are some of the ways coldframes can be used:

Rooting cuttings: Try softwood cuttings of geraniums, fuchsias, and chrysanthemums. Evergreen and semi-evergreen azalea cuttings will root within a month. (Take the current season's growth around mid-season before the wood has turned red or brown.) Many other deciduous and evergreen trees and shrubs are easily propagated by cuttings.

Early seed starting: Vegetable garden seeds and flowers can get started as much as eight weeks sooner in a coldframe.

Winter salad greens: In mild climates, a coldframe adds just enough extra warmth for the growth of lettuce, chives, and other salad greens right through winter. In cold climates, the same can be done in a well insulated coldframe. In some cases bottom heat may be necessary. (See *hotbeds,* page 78.)

Forcing: Early spring flowers such as primroses, pansies and candytuft can be forced into flower in pots placed inside a coldframe. Bulbs such as daffodils, hyacinths, and tulips can be coldframe forced.

This is the coldframe design so familiar to generations of gardeners. Ours was made of 2×12-inch stock, painted with a wood preservative to slow decay. The sash is glass. Sealant was used to prevent cold air drafts. The sloping roof is oriented to the south to maximize available winter sunlight.

Grandfather's Coldframe

Researching this story, we will read how coldframes, hotbeds, and other "season cheaters" were built and used in Grandfather's day. Here are the words of L. H. Bailey on coldframes, written in 1911:

"The common type of coldframe is twelve feet long and six feet wide, and is covered with four three-by-six sash. It is made of ordinary lumber loosely nailed together. If one expects to use coldframes or hotbeds every year, however, it is advisable to make the frames of two-inch stuff, well painted, and to join the parts by bolts and tenons, so that they may be taken apart and stored until needed for the next year's crop.

"It is always advisable to place coldframes in a protected place, and especially to protect them from cold north winds. Buildings afford excellent protection, but the sun is sometimes too hot upon the south side of large and light-colored buildings. One of the best means of protection is to plant a hedge of evergreens.

"There are three general purposes for which a coldframe is used: 1) for the starting of plants early in spring; 2) for receiving partially hardened plants which have been started earlier in hotbeds, and 3) for wintering young cabbages, lettuce, and other hardy plants which are sown in the fall."

Edward J. Wickson wrote in 1897:

"A coldframe is simply for the purpose of concentrating sun heat and protection from low temperatures and heavy rain storms. It is a convenient receptacle for seed flats, or it may be put over seeds sown in the ground. The frame is made of one-inch boards, the front board about twelve inches wide, the back board or boards eighteen inches wide and the sides sloping from eighteen to twelve inches to meet the widths of the front and back.

"The frame is usually made three feet from front to rear. This frame is then covered with glazed sash or cloth frames or lath frames or first one and then another, according to the amount of protection and heat or shade desirable. The arrangement is called a 'coldframe' because no provision is made for bottom heat. There are many modifications of the coldframe; lath or slat houses or lath covers for beds with raised edging boards, etc., etc., are all on the coldframe principle, and in warm climates where so little increment of heat is required and where shade is often desirable, the arrangement serves an excellent purpose."

Construction

The traditional cold frame is a rectangular box with a clear top that is angled to directly face the low winter sun. It is often made with a scrap lumber found around the house and either a glass sash or a plastic top.

For the frame, use 2×12 redwood or a wood treated with preservative. The back is made from two 6-foot lengths of redwood joined with 1×4 inches cleats spaced every four feet. Cut the two side pieces each 2 feet 8 inches long. When nailed inside the front and back lengths, this will allow the sash a 1 inch overhang to permit water runoff. To complete the ends, cut two more lengths 2 feet 8 inches long and saw diagonally from one corner to the other.

It is important that drafts do not circulate through the cold frame and either stunt or kill the seedlings. To minimize drafts, seal all the joints with a flexible sealant. Track weather stripping all around the frame where it joins with the sash. For even more protection, nail lengths of 1×4 inches around the front and the sides, allowing them to extend up flush with the top of the sash. Only the front, which overhangs for water runoff, cannot be further protected in this manner.

Put the top in place by hinging it in back so it can be raised or lowered for ventilation. On the front, use two hooks and screw eyes to keep it from blowing open in strong winds.

To support the sash when open, use hinges to fasten lengths of 1×1 inside. When the sash is closed, these will fold up and out of the way. The support stick is notched every four inches so it will fit snugly over a 16d nail driven in each end wall of the frame. This deep notching will both support the open top and yet keep it from blowing over backwards.

Instead of buying a glass sash for the cover of the cold frame, you can make one from either 2×2 redwood, or wood treated to resist the moisture buildup inside the frame. Like the glass sash, the top is three-by-six feet, with lap joints for an even fit all the way around. The two center braces are two feet on center apart. This will allow you to use lengths of clear corrugated fiberglass. The top can also be covered with clear plastic film to be replaced.

If you use corrugated fiberglass, use corrugated molding, either redwood or rubber, on the top and bottom to prevent drafts. Use aluminum nails with neoprene washers to fasten the fiberglass.

For glass covering, which will allow the maximum amount of light, use a router or dado saw blade to rabbet the edges of the frame ½-inch in and ⅛ inch deep. Lay a bead of sealant around the rabbeted edges before laying in each pane of glass. The glass is then held in place with strips of 1×2. Be sure and lay an additional bead of sealant around the edges of the glass before putting the strips in.

Raised Garden Covers

With raised gardens becoming more and more popular, there's no reason they can't be turned into mini-hothouses for an early start on your gardening season.

Build a redwood frame of 2×3 to fit directly on top of your raised bed. Use steel corners braces to strengthen it. Hinge one side of the frame to the raised bed, spacing the hinges every 2 feet to 3 feet apart. Now take a sheet of corrugated fiberglass and screw it to the hinged side of the frame. Use washers with the screws and pre-drill every hole 8 inches apart. Leave a ½-inch clearance around the bottom so the fiberglass will not hit the raised bed edge when the frame is tilted up.

Bend the fiberglass to the other side, making as near a half-circle as possible. Trim off any excess and then screw it to the frame. The ends are enclosed with ½-inch exterior grade plywood cut to fit snugly just inside the fiberglass. Glue a strip of molding to the fiberglass.

With this style, you can prop the whole frame up to work in the raised garden.

Above, one of our raised beds with a fiberglass coldframe on top. The protection it provided enabled a sweet potato crop to thrive where it is not well adapted. At 10 p.m., temperatures were 2 to 5° F. higher than the outside air. Ventilation was necessary in daytime.

A variation on this is to cover the plywood ends with foam molding and then screw the fiberglass to the ends —but only half way. With the screws going only to the top of the ends, one side can be flipped open for ventilation and access. When open, it is held with a hook and eye bolt in the rear of the frame.

If snow is a problem in your area, greater rigidity can be achieved by supporting the center with an additional end piece.

Hotbeds

A hotbed is a coldframe with the addition of bottom heat. In times past many more or less elaborate methods of supplying bottom heat were devised. Fermenting or composting organic matter was most common, but steam pipes, heated flues and similar systems were sometimes employed. Today of course, there are electrical and solar systems as well as traditional methods.

A hotbed more closely approaches the capabilities of a greenhouse. Many seeds only germinate readily when supplied with bottom heat. Cuttings of all types usually root more quickly.

This view of our fiberglass coldframe shows construction detail: fiberglass rather than solid ends for additional light; rubber cushions at the point the fiberglass sheet bends; hook and eye latch in the back holding the frame in an open position.

Raised bed, top and above, is planted to test nine carrot varieties. Fiberglass coldframe is secured to raised bed with hinges. Carrots are cold hardy but benefit with protection from wind, excess rain, and hail. Above left, coldframe removed from raised bed used to harden spring transplants.

Heat, How to Get It
Heat can be supplied to a coldframe in many ways. Following are descriptions of how to get the heat from organic matter, fires, electricity, and the sun.

Manure. Prior to the wide use of electricity, manure was the common way of supplying heat to a coldframe. There was a time when manure was a readily available resource and for many it still is. Horticultural writers to whom this practice was common are an excellent reference. We quote L. H. Bailey:

"It is important that the manure be as uniform as possible in composition and texture, that it come from highly-fed horses, and is practically of the same age. Perhaps as much as one-half of the whole material should be of litter or straw which has been used in the bedding. The manure is piled in a long and shallow square-topped pile, not more than four or six feet high as a rule, and is then allowed to ferment. Better results are generally obtained if the manure is piled under cover.

"The first fermentation is nearly always irregular; that is, it begins unequally in several places in the pile. In order to make the fermentation uniform, the pile must be turned occasionally, taking care to break up all hard lumps and to distribute the hot manure. It is sometimes necessary to turn the pile five or six times before it is finally used though half this number is ordinarily sufficient. When the pile is steaming uniformly throughout, it is placed in the hotbed, and is covered with the earth in which the plants are to be grown.

"Hotbed frames are sometimes set on top of the pile of fermenting manure. The manure should extend for some distance beyond the edges of the frame; otherwise the frame will become too cold about the outside, and the plants will suffer. It is preferable, however, to have a pit beneath the frame in which the manure is placed.

"Manure which has too much straw for the best results, and which will therefore soon part with its heat, will spring up quickly when the pressure of the feet is removed. Manure which has too little straw, and which therefore will not heat well or will spend its heat quickly, will pack down into a boggy mass underneath the feet.

"The amount of manure which is to be used will depend upon its quality, and also upon the season in which the hotbed is made. The earlier the bed is made, the larger should be the quantity of manure. Hotbeds which are supposed to hold for two months should have about two feet of manure, as a rule.

"The manure will heat very vigorously for a few days after it is placed in the bed. Use a soil thermometer that reaches into the manure to watch its temperature. When the temperature is passing below 90 F, seeds of the warm plants, like tomatoes, may be sown, and when it passes below 80 or 70 F the seeds of cooler plants may be sown."

As you can imagine, the manure heated hotbed entails considerable labor for a rather inexact result. How-

Left, the plastic cover on our raised bed gave lettuce early spring protection. Screen protected plants from birds. Right, fiberglass row cover gives tomatoes an early start. Heavy gauge wire controls width. Oval shaped row covers have proved superior to sharp angled types.

ever, properly prepared and handled as Mr. Bailey describes, it is a workable and reliable source of heat.

Horse manure is probably the easiest to handle but not required. Any fermenting organic matter is fine. For instance, a portable coldframe on top of a well prepared compost pile will benefit from the additional heat.

Flue-Heated Hotbed. This is another type of hotbed more complex but applicable to gardeners having a large supply of firewood or coal and desiring a large hotbed.

Picture the flue-heated hotbed like this: a fire pit at one end with 4-inch flues or stove pipes running the length of the bed. The hot gasses exit through chimneys at the opposite end. The chimney should be high in order to provide good draft. Generally, there should be a rise in the flues of at least 1 foot in 25. A steeper rise will insure good draft. The flue pipes should occupy a space beneath the beds and should never touch the bottoms of the beds unless insulated.

For a hotbed roughly 50 feet by 10 feet, lay three flues evenly spaced under the bed. The end closest to the fire box should be about 2 feet under the bed. The fire box end needs to be deeper to prevent that area from overheating.

For the fire pit, make it 4 feet square and about 4 feet deep. The fire box can be a 55-gallon drum on its side with three vent pipes welded on the back to connect into the three flue pipes. A door cut in the end with hinges welded on is the opening to feed the stove with wood or coal. An oil heater could also be used.

Start the first fires about three days before seeding to insure that the ground is warm enough. Check the temperature of the soil with thermometers. From then on, one fire in the morning and one in the evening should be enough to maintain warmth in the hotbeds.

Electric hotbeds. By far the simplest and most common method of heating a coldframe in use today is the electric cable. These are available in a variety of forms—with and without built-in thermostats, plastic and lead coated, and single or double wire. The "propagation mat" is probably the most convenient. It resembles the electric heating pad. With electric heat and a thermostat, precise control of bottom heat is obtained, therefore broadening the gardener's capability.

The length of soil cable to buy depends of course on the size of the area to heat. Also, same length cables from different manufacturers may have different capacities. As a rule of thumb, plan to use 2 to 4 linear feet of cable per square foot. For example, a 3×6-foot frame is 18 square feet. Depending on the manufacturer's recommendations, between 36 and 72 linear feet of cable will be required. Another way to determine how much cable you need is to allow 10 to 15 watts for every square foot. (In a sunny, wind-sheltered location, a well insulated hotbed would use only 10 watts.) Naturally, propagation mats heat an area equal to their dimensions.

Lay the cable on the level bottom of the frame, being careful not to overlap. If the cable is as stiff as a cold hose, plug it in and allow it to warm slightly. Also, clothes pins, or something com-

Day	Daily Maximum Temperature	Daily Minimum Temperature	Black and White 10p.m. clear	black	outside	Fiberglass Coldframe 10p.m. inside	outside	Automatic Coldframe 10p.m. inside	outside
1	95	49	66	68	60	62	58	64	60
2	86	48	62	63	58	59	55	60	57
3	77	54	59	62	57	60	55	59	57
4	73	56	60	61	58	62	58	61	59
5	70	54	63	64	60	61	58	62	60
6	77	51	65	67	63	64	61	65	63
7	82	49	67	69	63	64	61	65	63
8	89	56	62	64	58	64	60	60	58
9	84	50	65	66	62	65	59	62	60

parable, may help hold the cable in place. Then cover the cable with about an inch of sand. (Do not cover the cable with peat moss which may dry, insulate the cable, and cause it to overheat.) Hardware cloth or screen on top of this will protect the cable from hand tools. Directly on top of the screen, place a 5 or 6 inch layer of rooting medium such as sand, peat, or perlite.

For safety, be certain that all connections are moisture proof. Also, be sure that the assembly is properly grounded. A check with the local building inspector will determine if any special permits are required.

Solar heated hotbeds. Putting together two different ideas, our staff experimenters devised the solar heated bed shown on page 79. The solar panel we used is a commercially available type, intended for heating swimming pools. Eight ¾-inch plastic pipes were evenly spaced at the bottom of the bed. The direction of flow is from the top of the panel into the visible end of the bed. The 1¼-inch return pipe visible beneath completes the cycle.

We used it without pumps, relying on the rising hot water to give motion to the system. For this to function properly, we found it essential that all air be removed from the pipes, hence the hose spigots with which the system can be flushed.

The possibilities of a system such as this one are many. With the addition of a coldframe as shown on page 79, the solar heated hotbed is a reality. Some other basic solar heating techniques can help to transform the coldframe into a hotbed.

Line the outside of the frame with 1-inch thick pieces of rigid insulating material and extend this 12 inches into the ground. This insulating material will keep out the surface cold while trapping the natural warmth of the deeper earth.

Stack dark colored bricks against the back of the same on the inside. During the day these bricks will be thoroughly heated by the sun and during the night the stored heat within the bricks will slowly emanate back into the coldframe.

Large cans painted black and filled with water will do the same. For more on solar energy, see Chapter 7, page 53.

Test Garden Reports

Following are reports from our test garden in Los Altos, California. Here

Top, miniature greenhouse with dowel handle is a useful seed starter. Above, portable A-frame with plastic cover is an early spring row cover.

we conducted many experiments combining the coldframe/greenhouse principle with materials commonly available today.

The swing of temperatures and how to moderate them was the original question. We measured not only maximum and minimum temperatures, but also how many degrees each type of cold protection could provide.

New questions naturally follow old ones. Ways to utilize the simple principles of solar energy were explored as well as ways to speed seed germination.

We wanted to find out the following:

■ Will a coldframe make it possible to grow a vegetable crop (such as sweet potatoes) not well adapted to our climate?
■ Will a coldframe improve the setting of fruits on tomatoes and peppers?
■ How much frost protection will a coldframe provide?
■ What is the difference in reradiation between clear and black plastic? We knew clear plastic allowed unimpeded radiation to the plant and soil during the day. Theoretically, black plastic will slow reradiation to a cold night sky.
■ In what ways can we improve seed germination? We tried seed row covers (see page 74) and modified styrofoam picnic boxes.

On these pages are pictured some of our experiments. With soil and maximum/minimum thermometers, we kept track of temperatures both inside and outside of the "black and white" experiment, the fiberglass coldframe, and the automatic coldframe. The results are charted above on this page. The daily maximum and minimum are as reported by the local weather station. All temperatures are reported in degrees Fahrenheit.

Season Stretching Ideas—a Potpourri

Before using any kind of season stretching device, be it plastic jugs, plastic draped over an A-frame, a simple coldframe, there are a few things the gardener should know.

Where you use such early season growing aids such as row covers and plastic jugs is all important. In areas where temperatures are consistently cool, such aids fulfill their function very well. But if you live in an area

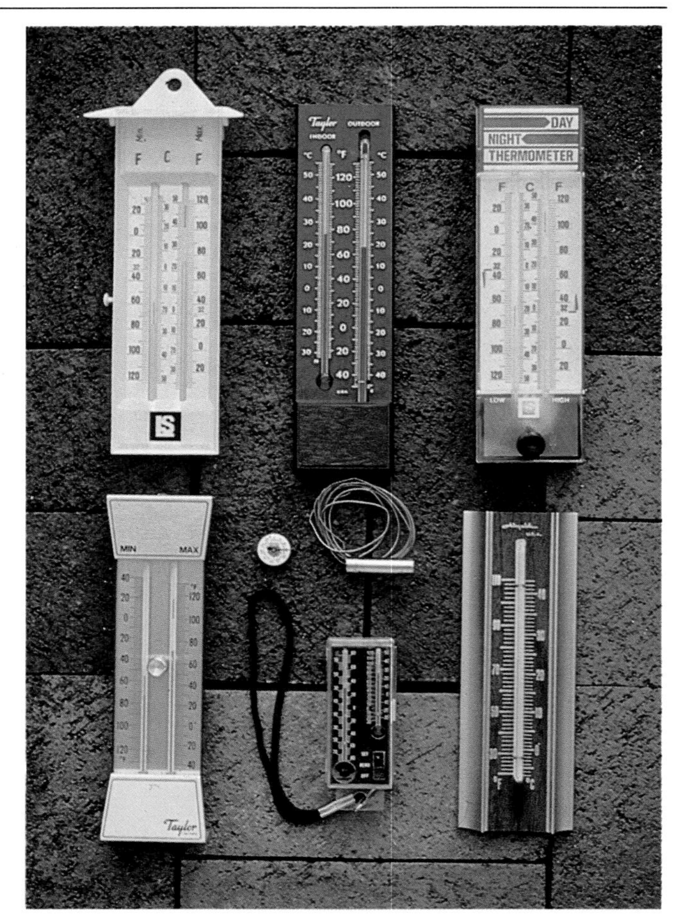

Above, in our "black and white" experimental planter, we were curious about differences between clear and opaque plastic mulches. One box was divided into two equal compartments. Under the clear side, temperatures were higher during the day and lower at night than the black side. At 10 p.m., soil temperature under the black side was 8 to 10 degrees warmer than the outside air. Right, we worked with several types of maximum/minimum thermometers. With a dozen in various locations, we were able to record garden microclimates. Temperatures varied from 60°F. against a brick wall to 52°F. near the ground.

where a stretch of cool spring weather may be broken by temperatures equal to a hot summer day, the gardener may find a plastic covered plant cooked to death.

Good ventilation is the key to avoid disaster. A row cover, with both ends open, should provide enough ventilation to allow the excessive heat to escape. If there is not ventilation through plastic covers of any kind, the covers should be removed on a warm day and replaced again at night.

In one of our test gardens we found a way to keep plastic row covers warm at night. We put large plastic bottles or plastic tubes filled with water inside the covers. During the day the sun warms the water. At night it slowly gives off heat and keeps the plants inside the cover a few degrees warmer. Remember, just slight temperature increases can make a considerable difference in plant growth.

The A-frame. The A-frame is an extension of the trellis idea. Vegetables that were once considered as space wasters in the small garden are now grown vertically. The small fruited watermelon, winter squash, melons and just about anything that vines can be trained skyward.

The A-frame can be positioned to take advantage of maximum sunlight and heat on one side, leaving the opposite for growing crops which demand a cooler environment.

It also can be converted into a tent for early spring frost protection. Try making a row tent out of the frame by covering it with plastic.

The "Hatch Patch"

Plastic mulches are proven season stretchers. They are particularly valuable for increasing yields and speeding up ripening of melons, eggplant, peppers and summer squash. In areas where early season temperatures are cool for these warm weather crops, yields of muskmelon in experimental plots have been increased up to four times using plastic mulch.

Duane Hatch, Extension Agent in Eugene, Oregon brings some of the Oregon State University research findings to the gardening public through the "Hatch Patch" demonstration garden. Here he reports on his experience with plastic mulches:

"A layer of plastic over the soil aids greatly with warm season crops such as tomatoes, melons, peppers and squash. The warming of the soil will promote 10 to 14 days earlier maturity and higher yields with tomatoes. Melons, seeded about the 10th of June gave us ripe cantaloupe and watermelon by mid-September.

"We demonstrated that clear plastic is better than black plastic because the sun's energy is expended on the soil rather than on the top part of the plastic. The weeds were not a major problem under the clear plastic if temperatures of 90° or more occurred to burn off the weeds. In 1974 we weren't getting enough heat to burn off the weeds, and we had to lift the plastic and do some hand weeding.

"The hills of squash and melons were planted through an X cut in the plastic. With the amount of water that goes through the planting hole and around the edge of the plastic, no special watering was necessary."

Above, we wondered if our plant display "staircase" could be converted into a coldframe/ greenhouse. The answer was a tentative yes. We found some growth improvement, probably due to wind protection and light dispersal. However, temperatures were not significantly improved and were, on occasion, 1 to 2 degrees cooler. Left, four tomatoes are supported by wire cages and covered with clear plastic, adding warmth in early spring. Bottom left, we found that the highest temperatures were maintained by switching from clear plastic during the day to black at night.

In another experimental planting in Oregon several tomato varieties were tested. We quote here from the Oregon Vegetable Digest:

"In 1973, 13 tomato varieties were tested at the North Willamette Experiment Station for their adaptability to the northern Willamette Valley.

"One of the growing beds was covered with black polyethylene plastic (1½ mils thick). Three plants of each variety were set 4 feet apart in the center of the bed. For irrigation, a porous wall tube ("Viaflo" by DuPont) was placed on the bed surface near the plants. Tubing was placed beneath the plastic mulch. A hole cut in the mulch permitted plants to be set. Plants were tied to a trellis of woven wire which was installed soon after planting.

"Earliest tomatoes were from unmulched plants, but the yield of marketable fruit from plants grown with the plastic mulch was increased by an average of 114 percent over that of unmulched plants. In addition, plastic mulch also increased fruit size an average of 13 percent, saved on irrigation, and prevented weed growth."

This commercial coldframe opens 6 to 7 inches when air temperatures exceed 72°F. It closes at air temperatures of 68°F. and below. No electricity is required—the automatic device is a simple thermocouple.

A styrofoam picnic box can be instantly converted into a miniature greenhouse. We have used the box for seed propagation. Nighttime heat retention is outstanding.

Hot Caps

These are another means of providing plants with the protection of controlled climates. They are excellent in areas where plants are in the ground and coming up but are still subject to snap freezes late in the spring or early fall.

The easiest hot cap is made by simply cutting off the bottom of a one gallon plastic milk jug. Leave the cap off during the day and replace it at night. If the day is warm, however, check the covered plants periodically. Heat can quickly build up even with the top off and cook young plants.

There are larger structures that will trap the sun's heat during the day and protect against frost at night. They do not have to be elaborate to be efficient.

A simple one is nothing more than a large clear plastic bag supported by four sticks over a plant. Sheets of polyethylene film draped over wire frames stuck in the ground and anchored with rocks will help provide a greenhouse effect for young plants. If the plant is entirely covered be sure to cut several vents in the plastic to prevent the plant from baking.

To cover rows at a time, bend 4×8 foot sheets of clear corrugated fiberglass and stake it at the sides. At night for added protection, drape the ends with polyethelene film or cut end blocks from plywood to fit. Tests were recently made with this type of cover to see if increased temperatures at early evening would speed the growth of peppers. The panel was put in place at sunset and removed the next morning. Soil and air temperatures checked at 11 p.m. nightly were higher than those in open rows and these covered peppers grew faster and larger than the exposed peppers.

The plant or row cover was widely used in England and France around the turn of the century. They used glass bell jars and called them a *cloche*. A simple *cloche* is two panes of glass clipped together at the top. Devise your own or obtain clips made specially for this purpose from suppliers of gardening equipment.

Shady Retreats

While plants need sunshine for maximum growth, a great many are too delicate for extended exposure to direct sunlight. An ideal answer is the lath house, a cool and shady retreat where plants can receive a proper balance of light and fresh air. Many lath houses also quickly become retreats for people who enjoy being outside yet protected from the direct rays of the sun.

Those sun-baked patios that are often too hot or too wet to use during summer days can be converted into gardens of filtered light with a variety of shade structures. The shade possibilities range from simply extending the roof line of your house to building a complete shade/lath house that becomes a place for both people and plants to refresh themselves.

In building a shade structure, most people cover it with wood strips because they are both aesthetically pleasing and long lasting. Lath is the standard cover, but you can use grape stakes or 1×2 firring strips which are effective and cheap. When you move up to 2×2 or greater in size for covering, your costs will go up sharply.

You might also consider having fewer lath strips overhead and using a bamboo screen or saran cloth for those really hot days. Saran cloth, generally used to shade greenhouses, will screen anywhere from 30 to 90 percent of the sun, depending on how tight the weave. In areas where excessive summer rain limits outdoor activities, shade structures can be covered with polyethelene or fiberglass.

Just how much shade you want and how large a shade structure you need depends on your personal taste. Here are some ideas to consider:

Laths, from the simplest to the most complex, can provide the extra climate modification for changing a harsh environment into a comfortable one.

Lath House

One of the most attractive additions to a yard is the lath house, either free standing or attached to an existing structure. It should be built with the idea that it will be a summer retreat not only for the plants but for people. Make it large enough for a table and chairs because when you hang it with plants, you and your friends are going to want to sit down and enjoy the new atmosphere. The roof can also be covered with panels of corrugated fiberglass to add the benefit of rain protection and extend its use where the climate is unpredictable.

The simplest and most practical variety of lath house is one attached to your house. Not only will its shade modify the climate for your plants but for your house as well. This attached structure should be built with two considerations in mind. First, the roof should be sloped slightly so that if you later cover it you will have runoff. A ¼-inch drop per foot is generally sufficient. Secondly, if you want to catch the sun to help heat the house during the winter months, then the roof and sides should be built in removable modules.

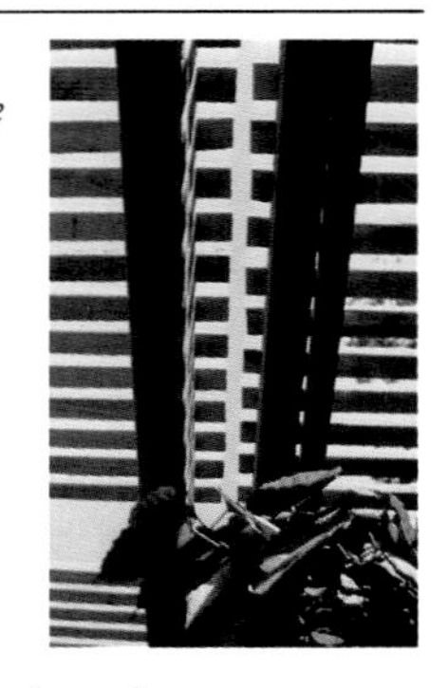

Details of lath construction. Removable lath sections with 2×2-inch end brace fit snug against 2×6-inch joist.

Here's how one lath went up on a south facing deck that was too hot and exposed during hot summer days. It was also designed so that the lath could be removed during the winter.

A concrete footing for the deck was already in place for the four redwood 4×4 posts that would be the outside supports. Using a concrete bit, holes were drilled at the measured points and steel post anchors were fastened with ½-inch expansion bolts. The uprights were put in place and bolted to the sides of the deck for additional bracing.

The shade porch rafters were attached to the house with 2×6 joist hangers on the barge board. These 16-foot rafters were attached to the posts with ½×4 lab screws. The rafters extended 4 feet beyond the posts for additional sun protection.

With the skeleton in place, a double row of 2×2s were nailed on top of the rafters 12 feet out from the house. This ties the unit together and minimizes any swaying.

The removable shade panels were made by nailing 1×2 firring strips onto 2×2s spaced just the width of the rafters. Each panel is light enough for one person to handle.

The removable lath sections are easily handled with help from a friend. Right, detail shows attachment of 4×4 support post to pier.

The western end of this lath house admitted too much late afternoon sun for comfort during the summer months. To counter this, panels similar to those on the rafters were built, but with the stops running vertically to give the impression of more height. These panels were simply screwed in place during the summer and then removed in the winter along with the overhead panels to admit more sunlight.

In the more likely event that you will have to put in your own foundation for the shade porch, you can use precast concrete piers or pour your own footings. These should be spaced 4 feet apart and if you pour your own, embed steel anchor posts in the concrete while still wet.

Once the footings are dry (at least 48 hours) put the 4×4 posts in place and bolt the bases to the anchor straps. Provide temporary bracings with 2×4s.

Instead of clasping each upright between two 2×6s as in the previous example, run a 4×4 bond beam across the top of all the posts. The posts should be cut so that when the bond beam is in place, the rafters will be sloping slightly away from the house for runoff in the event you later want to cover it.

The bond beam is best tied to each post with a steel T-brace. Once it is in place, extend the rafters and toenail them to the bond beam. Finally nail on the shade strips of your choice.

Attached shade structures offer two distinct advantages. First, the house wall gives excellent support, eliminating half the posts needed. Also, it is more convenient to use since the porch becomes an extension of your house. It is recommended that all shade structures be built at least strong enough to support the weight of a person. Anticipate the possible addition of solid roofing at some later date.

The tops do not all have to be covered with laths, particularly if you are in an area where direct, hot sunlight is not a real problem. You might also consider the egg crate construction which gives the sense of overhead protection but keeps it very open. An excellent way to create the egg crate effect is to lap joints wherever overhead pieces cross. It takes time to cut and chisel out each lap joint but the structure will go together quickly and with great strength. The alternate method is to lay out the stringers every 2 to 3 feet apart and then toe nail in each cross piece. Egg crate overheads can quickly be covered with bamboo screens, shade cloths or fiberglass panels later if more protection is needed. The open egg crate style also lends itself well to supporting natural coverings such as grape leaves.

Opposite page and left, an airy lath covered patio. Right, fiberglass covering.

Greenhouse Projects

Propagating plants from seeds or cuttings.
Terrariums and window greenhouses.
Lemons year-round.

Green Thumbs

After the smells of bleach and paint have left your greenhouse, it's time for the true gardener in you to come out. Nothing is so encouraging as success, so start with seeds or cuttings of some easy-to-grow plants, observe them and learn about your greenhouse as the plants grow, and share the results with your friends.

There's one maxim that all true growers, whether amateur or professional, must learn: Always give away (or sell) your choicest specimens. That may seem hard to do at times but it helps develop your ability to care for the remaining plants and bring them to perfection as well.

Propagation by Seeds

Nature's primary method of reproducing plants is with seeds. Far and away, most seeds that you purchase to grow in the greenhouse need only planting, constantly moist soil around them, gentle warmth (55° to 75° F, or 13° to 24° C) and light to become healthy seedlings.

All seeds must absorb water before they can start to grow, so overnight soaking in warm water will always speed the germination of seeds you buy. But it will also make very small seeds harder to sow because they'll tend to stick together.

For almost all seeds, a good soil mix is as shown on page 43 in Chapter 4.

How deeply should you plant the seeds? A good rule is not more than twice their thickness. If seeds are lost or germinate poorly, it is almost always because they were planted too deeply or because the soil was not kept uniformly moist. Plant the seeds in rows and label the rows if you're not sure you'll be able to identify the seedlings. You'll find that the weed seeds in the seed packages you buy are likely to appear first. Pluck out these seedlings as soon as you're sure they are weeds.

Once you've planted, don't be impatient; don't go poking around in the soil. The gardener's cardinal virtue is to leave everything to its own time and season. The seeds of some plants will germinate in five to seven days while others, like common parsley, may take three weeks.

You may want to grow seedlings from the seeds of trees or shrubs in the neighborhood. Then you'll want to be able to identify good ripe seeds and also know where the parent plants originated.

Above, propagating box maintains high humidity for seed germination or cuttings. Opposite page, grooming of prayer plant, Maranta leuconeura.

A seed has three basic parts:

1. The coat, which keeps moisture out to prevent permature germination.
2. The food storage to give the seedling a good start.
3. The embryo or tiny immature plant, which you can usually see at one end of a seed when you open it.

A few seeds with very hard coats are helped by filing or nicking them gently so that moisture can enter and trigger the germination process.

If the parent plant originated in the tropics, there's a good chance that the seeds will germinate almost as soon as you plant them in the greenhouse. But if the plant is native to a cold or temperate zone, you may have to simulate the cold springtime the seeds would have gone through in their natural setting. Storing the seeds for about forty days in a household refrigerator at about 40° F (4° C) will break the dormant period. The seeds should be mixed with a little slightly damp perlite, put in an open container and stirred every few days during their stay in the fridge. Then plant them as you would any other kind of seed in the greenhouse.

Transplanting a seedling once or twice before you give it a permanent home can help it develop a strong root system. In effect, you prune the roots each time you transplant, thus demanding less of the foliage while—in some plants—encouraging new roots to grow.

Propagation Without Seeds

We can imagine a person in the Stone Age bringing back some fruit-laden branches to the family, shoving the branches in the ground and smiling when the tribe passed that way the next year and saw that some of the branches were bearing fruit again. The planting of cuttings is an ancient way of propagating many trees and vines. The Middle East is also the native region of the olive, grape, pomegranate, date and many other fruit-bearing plants that can be grown from cuttings or "slips" of stems or roots.

When we know enough about the hormones and their combinations needed to promote the growth of roots, we may be able to propagate every species of plant without planting a seed.

For the present, it's helpful to consider some general rules that govern the ease or difficulty of getting cuttings from a stem to take root:

1. The younger the cutting, the more likely it is to root. Cuttings from most plants should be taken from shoots that are less than a year old. There are a few exceptions, such as the olive, that may do better if the cutting is from second-year wood.
2. It seems that the nearer the root the young cutting is taken, the better are the chances that it will in turn take root.
3. The larger the mature size of a tree, the less likely a cutting will take root. Again there are exceptions to this rule, such as poplar and willow which root fairly easily. And indeed, some experts have been able to grow the California coast redwood from cuttings.
4. The more leaves on a cutting, the better it will root because some of the most important plant hormones are produced in the margins of the leaves and at the growing points of the foliage. On the other hand, if the leaves are numerous and large, they'll give off more moisture than the cutting can take in and it will die.
5. The more light the cutting gets, the faster it will root as photosynthesis builds up the carbohydrate. Of course, too much direct hot sunlight will shrivel it up even faster.

Most Sedums *in moist sand a few days readily form roots, then tiny, new plants. Technically, these are leaf cuttings.*

The rooting medium can be almost any mix that has good drainage and lets oxygen penetrate, yet retains moisture. It should also be sterile if possible and support the cuttings well. Horticultural Peralite is one commercial product that seems to fill the bill. For greater moisture retention or a lower pH, add some ground sphagnum plant. Commercially available rooting hormones can benefit some plants but a great many plants produce enough hormones on their own. (The hormone compounds you buy are organic and rather unstable. Keep them in a closed container and away from light, preferably in a freezer.) If you notice that the bottom of a cutting is turning black, chances are that the rooting hormone is too strong.

Just where to take a cutting and how to handle it depends on the type of plant, as we describe below. But a good general plan is:

- Take a 4-inch cutting from a young wood.
- Strip the leaves or needles from the lower half, and cut across any very large leaves in the upper half.
- Bury the lower part 2½ inches deep in perlite or soil mix.
- Water once or twice a day, or use a misting system if your greenhouse has one.
- Keep in a place that gets about half total light (about 2,500 foot-candles) at around 60° to 65° F (16° to 18° C).

The surrounding temperature can be cooler if you have a heating cable that can keep the bottom of the seedling bed at about 70° to 75° F (20° to 23° C).

Here's a useful classification of cuttings:

I Stem Cuttings
- A. Hardwood
  - (1) Deciduous
  - (2) Narrow-leaved evergreens
- B. Semihardwood
- C. Softwood
- D. Herbaceous

II Leaf Cuttings
- A. Single leaf and petiole
- B. Leaf-bud

III Root Cuttings

Stem Cuttings

Cuttings are considered to be ***hardwood*** when they come from shoots that have grown through an entire season and the mother or stock plant is approaching or in a dormant period. The plant cells are fully formed and lignification—strengthening into woody tissue—has taken place. Of all the types of cuttings, the hardwood is the least likely to dry out, get wounded or fall sick before you can plant it.

Not all ***deciduous*** flowering shrubs can be propagated from stem cuttings but a surprising number can. One technique is to take the cuttings in the fall—just after the leaves have dropped—from shoots that grew during the spring and summer of that year. Discard the top 10 or 12 inches because this wood is not likely to be fully mature. Then cut the remainder in 12-inch lengths and as you gather up the lengths, be sure you keep them all running in the same direction (one easy way is to cut the bottom of each piece at an angle and the top straight across). Each length should have several nodes —the junctures where the leaves were joined to the stem —discard those that don't. Scratch or slice the bark up 2 or 3 inches from the bottom and, if you have some, rub a little rooting hormone compound into these wounds. Then tie about 10 to 25 cuttings in a loose bundle, remembering to keep them all pointing the same way, and label each bundle. Pack the bundles of cuttings loosely, bottom ends *up*, in a 5-gallon or other container that is 5 or 6 inches deeper than the cuttings and has many drainage holes in the bottom. Then fill the container with coarse perlite, set it in a cool place away from the light—under a bench, perhaps—and water it once or twice a week.

If you take the cuttings in November or December, they should be ready to plant by mid-February. Most species will be well-healed by then, some may already show roots and a few may even have some white top growth. Plant the cuttings in pots or trays about 6 or 8 inches deep and 6 inches apart, and put them in a cool place with plenty of light. As the spring gets warmer and days get brighter, move the containers into a shady location outside. By July or August you'll have a nice lot of young shrubs to replant in the garden.

The ***narrow-leaved evergreen*** hardwood cuttings are among the easiest to grow. These are the yews, junipers, arborvitae, cypress and some cedars and pines. But remember the general rule that the larger the mature plant, the harder it is to root the particular species or variety.

Take shoots from the past season's growth, discard a few inches of the less mature wood at the tip, cut the rest into lengths of about 4 inches, dip the lower half in a rooting hormone and plant about 2½ inches deep in perlite. If you have a heating cable, set it at 65° to 75° F (18° to 24° C) and place the cuttings' container on it. Water daily. In ten to sixteen weeks, most of the cuttings should be rooted, but wait patiently if they're not. Then transplant them either into a transplant bed, leaving 6 inches between each, or in pots. They should grow into nice bushy little plants in their first summer and can be transplanted to their permanent places in the second or third summer.

The cuttings of ***semihardwood*** plants are perhaps the most difficult to handle. These are the hollies, evergreen viburnums, rhododendrons, azaleas and other plants that do not lose their leaves in the winter. The first and biggest problem is to get cuttings of the right maturity. At least you can experiment: Take a few cuttings from the tips of branches every week and watch for rooting; you should then be able to decide which growth from the mother plant seems best for the variety and your area. If the tip of the branch snaps when you bend it, the wood is probably too mature. If it bends double without breaking, it's probably not old enough and will start to wilt as soon as you put it in the rooting mix. Try to choose shoots that are plump and have full-sized leaves. If the species has large leaves, cut away half of some of them. Follow the rooting procedure described above for narrow-leaved evergreens. Even if the old stock plant from which you took the cutting is perfectly hardy, its youngsters will need the protection of a greenhouse or cold frame during their first winter.

The ***softwood*** cuttings are the quickest of all to take root—or to die. Swedish ivy can take root in a week or less and many other houseplants need only two or three weeks. Get the cutting quickly from the stock plant into the rooting mix; a bit of rooting hormone powder may help but is usually not needed. If the cutting has a lot or very large leaves, remove some. Regular watering is essential and fertilize the cuttings with a good houseplant food or manure tea.

The last type of stem cuttings, the ***herbaceous,*** is actually two groups—the perennials and plants that have fibrous or succulent stems. Cuttings from plants in the latter group—the succulents, cacti and geraniums—have to be air dried so that the cutting wound will start healing before they are planted. Geraniums need about half a day and the succulents and cacti two or three days exposed to air but not to the sun. After planting, be careful not to overwater a succulent or cactus—just once every week or two is enough.

An herbaceous perennial is a plant whose top dies down in winter but its roots live on. Cut shoots that are 6 to 8 inches high from the stock plant at ground level and root them in perlite or a mix as if they were softwood cuttings. As soon as they are well-rooted, they can be transplanted directly to the garden.

Heat from electric cables speeds rooting of most cuttings.

Leaf-bud cuttings of schefflera, Brassaia actinophylla.

Leaf Cuttings

African violets, some of the begonias and some other plants can be rooted from a single leaf, which has to grow shoots as well as roots. Most plants that have this ability are characterized by thick fleshy stems and leaves covered with fine hairs.

Begonias will root from a leaf petiole (stem) or from breaks in the veins of a leaf if it is laid flat on the rooting mix and pegged down with a toothpick. When two little leaves have formed on the parent leaf, you will see tiny rows of red or black spots on their underside. These are the root initials and should be put down in the soil mix about ¼ inch. A good mix for these kinds of plants is half perlite and half potting soil. They should be lightly fertilized after a week or ten days.

The African violet and gloxinia take a little longer but usually root easily. Drops of cold water will mark their leaves so be careful when watering and don't expose them to mist. If you don't need many new plants, you can root these leaves in a glass of water and move them to pots as soon as you see the little plantlets form at the base of the leaf stem.

Some philodendrons can be easily rooted from a leaf that includes a bit of the branch it was attached to. Sometimes this is called a mallet or club cutting because that's what it looks like. Be sure not to plant such a cutting more than 1½ inches deep, then care for it as you would a softwood cutting.

Root Cuttings

We don't usually see the roots of a plant so we often don't study them or think of them as cuttings. But in fact, almost any species of plants that grow out of the ground in 2 or more stems can be rooted from roots. This is an especially good method for lilac and quince, which can't easily be rooted from stem cuttings.

The best time to take root cuttings is just before an active period of growth, usually very early spring. Dig up the mother plant or part of it to get the cuttings, then replant the parent. Cut lengths of root of 3 or 4 inches from just under the ground's surface and be sure to keep the top end up when you plant them in rows about ¼-inch under the surface of the rooting mix. Keep them watered and a few weeks later you should see the shoots coming through the mix.

Above and right, plants for the vegetable garden, such as corn and cucumbers, are easily started from seed. Middle, plastic top for flat of leaf cuttings. Bottom, ferns started from spores enclosed in plastic bag.

Terrariums

Terrariums are the bottled jewels of indoor gardens. They range from exquisite miniatures inside pill bottles to fully landscaped gardens inside fish tanks. Terrariums are ideal for plants that require warmth, high humidity, and ideal soil conditions.

There is really no limit to what can be planted in terrariums. Even cacti will grow under glass if planted in a sandy soil and kept dry. But most plants are selected for their small size, tropical nature, and slow growth.

History

Both the Phoenicians, who were linked to ancient Semitic cultures, and the Greeks had the legend that Adonis, the slain lover of the Greek goddess of love Aphrodite, was brought back to life each year. In this festival of Adonis, the Greeks celebrated the mystical cycle of death, life and death. As part of the celebration, the Greeks created tiny "gardens of Adonis" where plants were grown from seed in pots or baskets, sealed for eight days, then thrown into the sea as a symbol of the death and rebirth of all vegetable life. These were the ancestors of the terrariums we have today.

This latest great epoch of terrariums began in 1829 with Dr. Nathaniel Ward, a surgeon with an interest in natural history. He was studying the life cycle of the sphinx moth in sealed jars. Within a few days he noticed condensation running down the sides of the bottle and shortly thereafter was astonished to see tiny ferns sprout. The ferns lived four years in the bottle without a drop of water. In 1832 he packed ferns and moss into two large glass containers and sent them to Australia, eight months distant. They flourished, as did the plants that Australia shipped back under glass.

Dr. Ward immediately began producing what became known as "Wardian Cases." They were partly responsible for the movement of plants around the world to botanical gardens. The great tea plantations of northern India were established by a shipment of 20,000 tea plants from Shanghai in Wardian cases. All previous attempts to ship the plants alive had failed.

Planting the Terrarium

First, make sure the container is clean and completely dry. If it is a long necked bottle, leave it overnight or dry in the oven at a low temperature for a few hours. This will help prevent the soil from sticking to the insides when preparing to plant.

The first layer into the terrarium should be fine gravel or crushed rock for drainage. Excess water will flow into the gravel and keep your roots from rotting or drowning. Too much water is the common problem in terrariums.

On top of the gravel, add a fine layer of activated charcoal. Next, a thin layer of sphagnum moss to keep the soil from sifting into the gravel. Finally, add your soil mix through the funnel.

When placing the plants, whether in the bottle or open container, plant the largest ones first for two reasons: you will not dislodge the smaller plants that way, and arranging the larger plants first gives you a good focal point for the garden.

Prepare the hole with the stick. Then, using the grasping tool or wire, lower the roots into the prepared hole and tamp the plant in place.

Next, place any piece of driftwood, rock, or small statue that you might want in your garden. Add your additional plants, and finish with small pebbles.

Watering

After the garden is in place comes the critical task of giving it the right amount of water. The soil should be damp but not soaked. Excess water in a terrarium, particularly in a bottle, is difficult to get rid of because there is so little evaporation. You must have enough water to start the rain cycle in the bottle. This rain-forest effect will keep your terrarium lush.

Add lukewarm tap water carefully in order to not dislodge the plants. In open containers a fine-holed sprinkler can or mister will work fine. In bottles, tip the container slightly and let the water trickle down the sides, which will also wash away any soil stuck there.

If you have doubts, water less than you think you should. Watch the container. If condensation builds up in a few hours, the terrarium is probably all right. If you think you underwatered and the plants begin to droop in a day or two, add a little more.

Extreme fogging and condensation inside are signs of overwatering. If this happens, remove the top and let the excess moisture evaporate.

Maintenance

Once the proper rain-forest effect is established, your terrarium should be largely self-sustaining. It will probably not need water for one to two months. You will be able to spot its needs by lack of condensation and possibly wilting.

Lighting is vital to any successful garden, including the terrarium. In the winter months, keep the plants near windows so that they might receive all the light they need during the shorter days.

Reminders

Be sure to turn your terrarium periodically so that all sides receive equal amounts of light. This will keep the plants growing straight. Every month to six weeks, you can add a few drops of liquid house plant food mixed at one-fourth the listed strength for standard potted plants.

Fish-tank terrarium such as one shown is one of the easiest and best ways to exploit terrarium principal. Several varieties of ferns thrive with window exposure and supplemental fluorescent light.

Window Greenhouses

The window greenhouse is a big step up from gardening along a window sill. It is more than just putting plants in a bay window. A real window greenhouse closes on the inside so that the plants are not subject to the drying effects of the house. They are in their own greenhouse environment.

However, this can create a problem that you should be aware of. These little greenhouses are small and if enclosed on the inside, they can heat up rapidly when hit with sunlight. It can also cool markedly at night. Vents that connect to the outside and from your room into the window greenhouse are important to keep the air relatively constant. This is not a serious problem; however, it is one to be aware of.

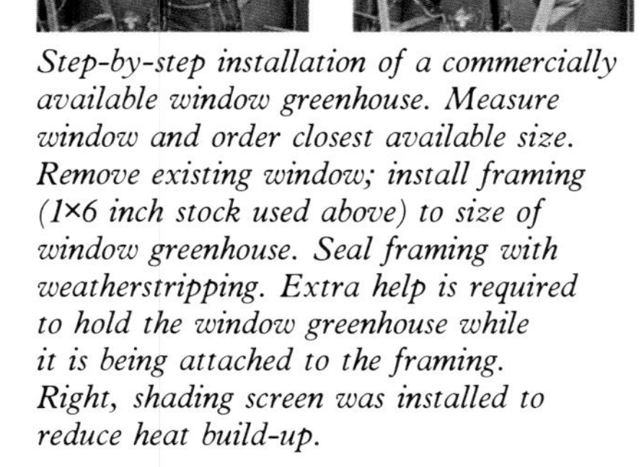

Step-by-step installation of a commercially available window greenhouse. Measure window and order closest available size. Remove existing window; install framing (1×6 inch stock used above) to size of window greenhouse. Seal framing with weatherstripping. Extra help is required to hold the window greenhouse while it is being attached to the framing. Right, shading screen was installed to reduce heat build-up.

Location

Almost any window in the house will do. It depends on the effect you wish to create and what plants you want to grow. To get maximum sunlight, especially during the winter months, the best location is a south-facing window. Next choice is the east which gets the morning and mid-day sun. A western window will get late afternoon sun only and one north-facing window will get minimal light unless you live in the deep south.

However, with the help of fluorescent lighting to give the plants any additional light they need, you can put a window greenhouse anywhere you wish—even into a bathroom window that opens into an air shaft in the midst of an apartment complex.

Once a window greenhouse is installed, the room suddenly seems larger, more open and spacious. So put it where you think it will look the best and do the most for your room. Then, make it flourish with plants for that exposure.

Window Types

Before you start building the window greenhouse, or go out and buy one, consider what kind of window you have and how to remove it. The six basic types of window are awning, jalousie, fixed, casement, double hung and sliding.

The fixed awning and jalousie windows are normally in steel or aluminum frames. Simply unscrew and lift out.

To remove a double hung window, first pry loose the inside stop on one side of the window frame. With that out of the way, pull that side of the window toward you and out from the groove on the opposite side. Then lift out the sash cord.

For a casement window, first unscrew the crank and operating bar. Next unscrew all hinges on the inside of the window doors. To remove the steel casement frame, unscrew it on the sides, then remove the inside stops as for a double hung window and lift out.

If you want to remove the sliding window, first loosen the release screw at the inside top of the sliding window. Then lift up and pull out at the bottom. The fixed frame will come the same way, although it is fitted more tightly. In some instances you may have to remove the center frame piece.

Above, front and back views through silver screen. Silver coating on one side of shade cloth reflects heat. The fabric weave provides about 65 per cent shade. Hold it in place on the window with either two-sided adhesive tape or spray type adhesive. Silver screen is similar to a one-way mirror permitting visibility one direction and not the other.

The Tropicals

Since a greenhouse is a controlled environment, it's no trick to grow pineapple or papaya in Montana or Maine. Just plan ahead to have the exotic fruits you want for Thanksgiving or any other worthy occasion. Seeds are available from many seed companies or you can buy young tropical plants from nurseries in southern areas of the country.

Pineapples

This fruit is not the result of a union between a pine and an apple tree. Its name comes from the fact that it was once much smaller and resembled a pine cone.

To make a little pinery in your greenhouse, reserve a sunny spot for a 12-inch pot. Then buy a ripe pineapple at a fruit stand or your market. Twist rather than cut the top off and leave it to air dry for about a week in any warm, dry place. The pineapple is a bromeliad and the fruit will stay alive for many days after it's picked.

After the top has cured, plant it in very porous soil. A good mixture is 1/3 compost, 1/3 manure and 1/3 garden soil mixed in turn with an equal quantity of perlite.

When you see that the pineapple top has rooted and is beginning to grow, give it a little fertilizer. You can put about a tablespoonful of blood meal down in the center of the leaves or you can use any liquid plant food. If you use a liquid, sprinkle it generously over the leaves as well as the roots of the plant. In either case, be careful that you don't snap or injure the new leaves which are surprisingly brittle.

After about 18 months, the pineapple plant should be moved to a 12-inch container and kept in the warmest and brightest part of the greenhouse. At about 30 months, a lovely flower spike will shoot above the leaves. After it's gone, you'll see the little immature pineapple. The more food, water, warmth and light you can give the parent plant, the larger the fruit will grow. The plant is now strong enough to be shown off in the house for a day or two at a time. As the fruit comes of age it will turn slightly yellow and begin to get soft. Pick it when you can't stand the temptation any longer. The parent plant will continue to grow offshoots and suckers for several years. Keep on fertilizing and watering it, and your next crop may be two or three mouth-watering fruits. The plant will produce for six or seven years but the fruit will get progressively smaller.

Passion Fruit

Passiflora edulis is a beautiful vine to grow in a greenhouse, although it can stand a bit of frost. The seeds germinate easily. Sow them about ⅛-inch deep in regular potting soil. They will germinate in two or three weeks. When the second set of leaves appears, move the plantlet to a 12- or 14-inch tub that has a trellis attached. If you want a larger vine, transplant 3 of the seedlings in a 16-inch tub. The tub can be moved outside to a semishaded area each summer. The vine is not likely to flower the first year but should during the following winter in the greenhouse.

Lemons are among the most productive greenhouse fruits bearing year-round.

Passion fruit is seedy but delicious. Even without the fruit, the leaves and flowers make this easy-to-grow tropical splendor worthwhile.

Papaya

There's little comparison between store-bought and tree-ripened papaya. Only the finest and sweetest of our melons begins to approach the quality of this tree melon from the tropics.

The papaya is a very tender plant and must be kept constantly at temperatures of about 60° F (16 ° C) if you're to have a vigorous tree. Like other tropicals, it will thrive on nighttime temperatures of 70° to 75° (21° to 24° C). It will usually die if the temperature drops even for a short time below 40° F (4° C).

You can buy the seeds of many varieties of papayas but the easiest thing to do is to save the seeds from a fruit you've bought at the market. Wash them well in a strainer, and plant them immediately, following the procedure for passion fruit. A heavy application of organic fertilizer is fine at two-week intervals after the plant is well-started. Transplant upward to a 16- or 18-inch tub as the final container.

A papaya seed sown in January or February should produce fruit about 24 months later. The plant is lovely, growing straight and upright with the fruit appearing near the trunk just under the leaves.

Guava

Feijoa sellowiana is best purchased as a plant because the seeds are very small and sometimes difficult to germinate. Grown in a greenhouse tub, the guava will reward you with handsome gray green leaves that are nearly silver underneath, beautiful red and white flowers, and the small oval fruit.

The plant has to be pollinated. If you don't want to let a few bees in the greenhouse, you'll have to hand pollinate with a soft and small paint brush. Go from blossom to blossom, brushing the center of each with a couple of gentle strokes. Do this every other day until petals fall.

Citrus

Any of the endless varieties of citrus fruits you find in the market is available for greenhouse growing. Many citrus are on dwarf rootstalk and others are naturally small. Many of the best varieties are grafted so you'll have to buy the plants rather than planting seeds. If you have room for only one tropical fruit tree in your greenhouse, consider a dwarf lemon of a variety that will bloom and fruit year-round.

Growing citrus in a tub is different in only two ways from growing other greenhouse plants. First, the soil should not be kept constantly moist but instead it should be allowed to dry out at regular intervals in order to stimulate the roots. Don't let the plant wilt, though, and do give the foliage a good spraying with water regularly. Second, citrus plants need fertilizing monthly to produce good fruit. If the fruit is sour or the skin very thick, the plant has probably not been getting enough food.

Index